BARE
ESSENTIALS

BRAS

CONSTRUCTION AND PATTERN DRAFTING FOR LINGERIE DESIGN

PUBLICATION BY
LOS ANGELES FASHION RESOURCE
Fairbanks Publishing, LLC

Jennifer Lynne Matthews - Fairbanks

Book Design by Designarchy
Cover Photography by Ashley Burke
Interior Photography by David Fairbanks
Written by Jennifer Lynne Matthews-Fairbanks

Services for our readers:

Universities and wholesale purchasing:
The Los Angeles Fashion Resource offers special rates for universities and for wholesale purchasing.

Wholesale purchasing is available through Ingram Distributing or directly through the Los Angeles Fashion Resource.

Updates:
Information contained in this book was current at the time of publishing. For updates, check our website. www.LosAngelesFashionResource.com

Contact Us:
Los Angeles Fashion Resource
info@losangelesfashionresource.com

Your feedback is always welcome. Let us know if we can do anything to improve this title.

ISBN-10: 0983132844
ISBN-13: 978-0-9831328-4-4

CONTENTS

PREFACE

As a lingerie designer and educator, I felt there was a hole in educational texts for lingerie design. I compiled this information for educational purposes from personal experience and experimentation. This book series is designed to take an individual through the process of sewing lingerie, developing pattern modifications and drafting from measurements.

This book covers many different aspects of the design process and is divided into three basic sections As one progresses through the book, the directions become more complex, as to help each individual master the art of lingerie design.

Each step in the book has been tested by both students and educators to achieve the best possible information possible. If you encounter a discrepancy, please contact us so we will be able to update the book with the correct information. If you are unable to achieve our results, feel free to contact us regarding the issue. It may be a mistake on our part, or possibly we could help explain it more thoroughly. Feedback is always welcome and I thoroughly encourage it.

This book is volume two of the Bare Essentials series. The focus of this book is bra design. Check www.losangelesfashionresource.com periodically for updates on new books available from the series. Currently three additional volumes are planned, including active wear, lounge wear and mens undergarments. The first book in the series focuses on underwear design.

Enjoy your venture into designing and creating your own lingerie.

-Jennifer Matthews-Fairbanks

Jennifer Lynne Matthews-Fairbanks is an instructor at the Fashion Institute of Design and Merchandising in Los Angeles. She owns and operates her own lingerie design business, Porcelynne Lingerie, which has been in operation for the past 10 years.

A special thanks to my husband, David Fairbanks, for being there for me every step of the way. I would also like to thank Katie Sabo and my special projects class at FIDM for their help in the completion of this book.

BEGINNER

CHAPTER 1

INTRODUCTION TO LINGERIE CONSTRUCTION

Before entering a path into bra design, one should develop an understanding of bra construction and the materials used.

Each introduction chapter details the tools, supplies, notions and materials used for the projects in that section.

ANATOMY OF A BRA

There are three general parts to a bra: the cup, the band and the bridge.

Cup - A cup of a bra can be seamed or molded, with a variety of coverages: full coverage, demi cup, half cup or quarter cup. The high point of the cup is referred to as the apex or bust point.

A seamed cup contains one or more seams to shape the bust and is generally in a stable fabric without stretch. This seam can be horizontal, vertical, diagonal or any design of your choosing. The key is that one seam intersects the apex of the bust.

All seams on a bra should be shielded from the

body from irritation by either a lining or the use of seam tape. A seamed cup can also be padded.

A molded cup is another possibility, but as a designer or maker, you are generally limited in this area due to the specifications made by the manufacturer of the specific cup. Molded cups can be with or without padding.

Band - The band can be in multiple pieces, joining under the cup and/or at the side seam.

A band that contains a side seam generally has two distinct differences: the front band contains no stretch (and utilizes a stabilizer) and the back band is constructed of a stretch fabric such as

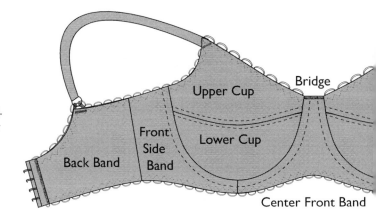

power netting. Larger cup sizes may contain a piece of boning at the side seam for additional support of the bust.

A band can also be constructed without a side seam. The entire band in this scenario would be constructed of a stretch material. The center bridge would need to be stabilized even if the entire band is constructed out of a knit.

Bridge - This is the center of the bra that connects the two cups together. The bridge can be incorporated into the band, it can be freestanding or it could be decorative in nature by using alternative materials in the construction. The bridge uses a stabilizer to keep from stretching out of shape.

TOOLS & SUPPLIES

If you are a seasoned sewer, you will most likely already possess many of these tools, but for those just starting out, this is a suggested shopping list.

Dressmaker Pins - There are a variety of different pins one can use in sewing. Some are very pliable and made from less than quality materials, while others are sturdy and strong. In the varieties available, make sure to get pins that are appropriate for what you are working on. Silk pins are recommended for delicate fabrics.

Because I have spilled over a box of pins more than once in my life, I recommend using a magnetic pin cushion over the traditional tomato.

For those of you that might be prone to farsightedness, you may wish to use pins with colored plastic on the end. Just be careful, you cannot iron over the colored balls or they will surely melt to whatever you are working on and ruin your iron.

Dot Paper - Dot paper is what we use in the industry for drafting. Although funny enough, the markings are generally not dots, but numbers and letters on a grid. Dot paper can also be referred to as alpha-numeric paper. This paper may not be available in all areas. Poster paper or craft paper can be used as acceptable alternatives. I prefer white poster paper for it's moderate transparency.

Fabric Shears and Scissors - The words shears and scissors can be interchanged,

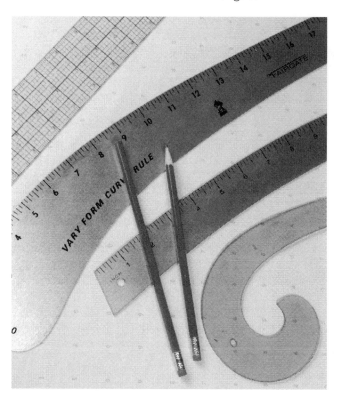

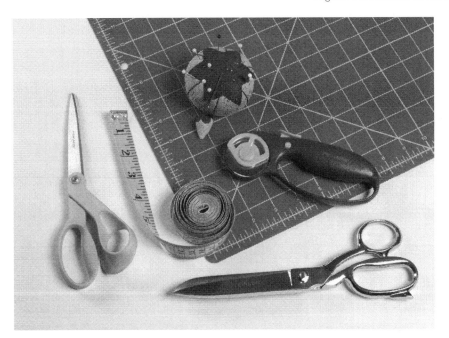

although shears is the industry standard term. Make sure to purchase a pair of quality shears and designate them for fabric use only. A good pair can cost a pretty penny, so make sure not to cut paper, hair or random household items with these scissors.

French curve - A French curve is used for making small and tight curved shapes, generally for armholes and necklines, but it can be used for other shapes as well. French curves are sometimes available in a variety pack containing multiple curved shapes.

Hip or Vary Curve - A hip curve or vary curve will be needed for longer and gradual curves, typically used for waistlines and side seams.

Paper Scissors - As one should have a pair of scissors specific to fabric, a pair specifically for cutting paper products is also necessary.

Pencils - In order to get accurate shapes and edges, either use a mechanical pencil or a pencil with a very sharp point (or have a pencil sharpener handy). You may wish to have a few colored pencils handy to help differentiate pattern changes.

Rotary Cutters and Cutting Mats - When working with small and detailed designs, using a large pair of shears isn't always practical. Use of a rotary cutter or an exacto knife ensures a precise cut every time.

Make sure to use a cutting mat under whatever you happen to be dissecting. You don't want to destroy your dining room table. Cutting mats can be pricey, so choose a size that will be appropriate for your cutting needs. The use of rotary cutters and cutting mats is commonly used when cutting bras and delicate laces.

Straight See-Through Rulers - This will be important for your drafting. These are generally available in both the imperial and metric system.

For the imperial system, measurements are taken in 8ths. Because of the complexities of a bra, one should also reference 16th and 32nds. The table to the right lists the conversion of fractions to decimals. This chart may prove handy through this book.

Tape Measure - A soft tape measure is needed for taking your measurements or those of your fit model. Many tape measures have the imperial system (inches) on one side and the metric system (centimeters) on the other.

NOTIONS FOR BASIC BRA PATTERNS

A restricted variety of these items can be found at your local fabric store. For a more exclusive inventory of choices, there are many bra making resources available online. Our publisher carries a limited selection of these supplies for convenience of working with these books. www.losangelesfashionresource.com

Boning - Boning can be acquired in plastic or metal. For bra construction, plastic in a 1/4" or .6cm width is recommended.

Boning Casing - Casing is sometimes sold with boning as a set. To create your own casing, use a 1" or 2.5cm wide strip of soft woven fabric either straight grain or bias cut. Fold in both

IMPERIAL MEASUREMENT CONVERSION CHART
Measurements in Inches

1/32	0.03
1/16	0.06
3/32	0.09
1/8	0.13
5/32	0.16
3/16	0.19
7/32	0.22
1/4	0.25
9/32	0.28
5/16	0.31
11/32	0.34
3/8	0.38
13/32	0.41
7/16	0.44
15/32	0.47
1/2	0.50
17/32	0.53
9/16	0.56
19/32	0.59
5/8	0.63
21/32	0.66
11/16	0.69
23/32	0.72
3/4	0.75
25/32	0.78
13/16	0.81
27/32	0.84
7/8	0.88
29/32	0.91
15/16	0.94
31/32	0.97

edges 1/4" or .6cm and press to reveal a 1/2" or 1.25cm piece of casing.

Hook & Eye Tape - This tape generally has three columns of eyes for adjusting the fit as the bra stretches out. The hook & eye tape can contain one row or multiple rows. One row is used for small cups. The larger the cup and the larger the band, there may be a variation for the number of rows used for the bra. Strapless bras generally contain more rows for additional support.

Seam Tape - Seam tape is a thin piece of nylon mesh that is soft and is stitched over a seam to avoid irritation of the seam against the skin.

Sliders and Rings - Sliders are used for making a strap adjustable and resemble an "8." Rings are used to attach straps to the body of the bra and resemble an "O." Both are available in a variety of sizes based on the width of the strap elastic.

Straps - The straps can vary in width from 1/4" to 1" or .6cm to 2.5cm. Some straps are constructed using woven fabrics, some can include padding, but most are comprised of elastic. Straps contain a slider and a ring for adjusting fit and size.

Underwire - Underwires come in a variety of shapes and sizes. They generally come in full coverage or demi. If a design requires an underwire between the two sizes, one can either cut down a full coverage wire or create their own specs and have custom wires

manufactured. Underwires may be coated in nylon or are comprised of plain spring steel, but they always have capped ends to ensure that the wires do not poke through the bra.

Underwire Channeling - Channeling is used to encase the underwire around the cup. Because of the close proximity to your body, channeling has a brushed texture to it.

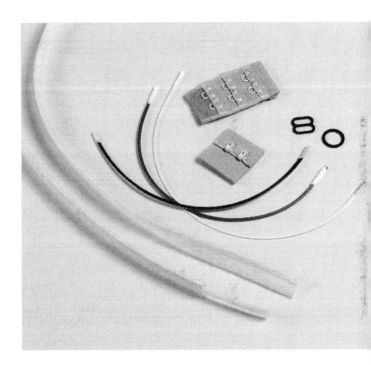

GUIDE TO FABRICS

Before elaborating too deeply into the variety of fabrics commonly used in lingerie design, here are the basics. Fabrics generally fall into two categories: woven and knit.

Woven Fabric - These fabrics are created by threads being intertwined from two different directions.

Knit Fabrics - These fabrics are created by a single yarn that is looped on a course. The yarn is pulled through loops to create a knit stitch on one side and a purl stitch on the other side. The knit side appears to look like lines of V's and the purl side is full of loops.

Every fabric has different characteristics. Many of these characteristics can be attributed to the grainlines of the fabric. The following is a brief summary explaining the grains of a fabric.

Selvage - The selvage of a fabric is the finished edge of the fabric that runs down the length of the fabric.

Length Grain - This refers to the length of the fabric. This grain is parallel to the selvage and is what we call the warp grain in the fashion industry. It can also be referred to as the straight grain. For simplicity sake, I will use the term length grain when referring to this direction.

Cross Grain - When a fabric is woven, the threads on the length grain are generally stationary and a weft thread (as we call it in the industry) is woven back and forth from edge to edge creating the finished selvage. This weaving action causes the weft grain of the fabric to have more pliability than the straight grain. The weft or cross grain of a knit is the stretchiest part of a knit fabric.

Bias - The bias of a fabric is the stretchiest option when using a woven fabric. Bias is a 45 degree angle from the length grain. Using the bias on a knit fabric is not recommended

because it does not provide for additional stretch and it unnecessarily creates fabric waste.

FABRICS FOR BRAS

The following fabric can be used with the patterns provided in this book. When creating your own patterns, other fabrics can be incorporate into your lingerie designs, but the patterns will vary based on their stretch. The Advanced section delves deeper into the subject of stretch.

Jersey Knits - The most common knit is known as a jersey knit. Jersey knits are found on everyday clothing such as tee shirts and underwear.

Power Net - This is generally a nylon/spandex net mesh. It is used on the back band; it has a firm stretch and a great recovery. Stretch fabrics other than power net can be used for the back band, but tend to stretch out more than a band constructed with power net.

Spandex Knits - This knit is a jersey knit with Lycra® or spandex fibers that allows for more stretch. This fabric is recommended over a plain jersey knit for bra construction and is sometimes used in replacement of power net.

Stabilizer - This fabric is sheer, rigid and should not stretch. It is generally a nylon net and is used on the front band and center bridge of a bra. If this fabric contains a stretch, cut the required pattern pieces on the cross grain to restrict stretch across the body. Stabilizer cut in strips can be used as an alternative to seam tape.

Lace Fabric - Laces can be created by both woven and knit construction. Depending on the stretch of the lace, the lace can be treated as either. Woven lace is recommended for cup construction. Knit laces are recommended for the back or areas of stretch.

MACHINES & STITCHES

For general purpose use, this book has been developed with illustrations referring to stitches found on a basic home sewing machine and serger.

HOME SEWING MACHINE

When constructing a bra, a combination of knit and woven fabrics are used. You will need to use the most appropriate stitch for the fabric in question.

WOVEN FABRIC

Straight Stitch - This stitch is needed when constructing the cup and attaching encasements for underwire and boning.

Double Needle Stitch - This stitch is formed with two needles on the top. The top of the stitch contains two straight stitches, while the back appears as a zigzag. This stitch isn't necessary, but could be helpful when applying seam tape to the cup.

Bar Tack Stitch - This stitch is a very tiny zigzag stitch and can be done on most sewing machines. This stitch will be used when attaching the straps, hook and eye closures and at the ends of the channeling for the underwire.

Most home machines have zigzag functionality to them. The setting for this stitch will be similar to that of sewing a buttonhole. The spacing between is usually very small and the width is narrow.

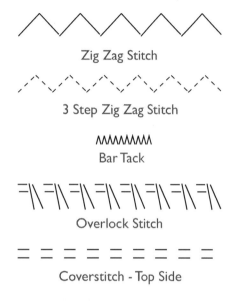

Zig Zag Stitch

3 Step Zig Zag Stitch

Bar Tack

Overlock Stitch

Coverstitch - Top Side

Coverstitch - Back Side

KNIT FABRIC

One should avoid using a straight stitch when sewing stretch fabrics and elastics. If a stretch material is sewn with a straight stitch and the fabric stretches beyond the length of the stitch, the thread can break causing a garment to unravel.

Zigzag Stitch - The zigzag stitch is the recommended stitch for sewing stretch fabrics. It allows the fabric and elastic to stretch without threads breaking.

Three Step Zigzag Stitch - This is my favorite stitch when constructing lingerie. It allows for stretch and it also secures the thread

in the stitch better than a traditional zigzag.

Decorative Stretch Stitches - A home machine may do additional stitches that allow for stretching. Test each decorative stitches by sewing in the stretch direction of a knit fabric and then pull the fabric to see if the stitches break or move with the fabric.

SERGER SEWING MACHINE

A serger is also referred to as an overlock. This machine is ideal for sewing stretch fabrics. It cuts the edge of the fabric off while stitching. It generally has 4 threads to it, two reinforce the seam and two threads form an overcast on the edge of the fabric, leaving a clean finished edge.

Specialty Stitches - Depending on which model you own, home serger sewing machines can sometimes do specialty stitches such as a coverstitch or blind stitch.

INDUSTRIAL SEWING MACHINES

Industrial machines come in all shapes and sizes. They are great for production, but unfortunately, a different machine is needed for every type of stitch.

Straight Stitch Machines - These do just one stitch with a back stitch. You can get a buttonhole attachment for this machine for more versatility.

Zigzag Machine - This does just that- a zigzag.

Three Step Zigzag Machine - The perfect lingerie stitch.

Overlock Machine - These machines can vary from 3 to 5 threads. 5 threads provides a safety stitch (which isn't practical for stretch fabrics). The 3 thread is more common in lingerie design because of the size of the stitch.

Coverstitch Machine - A coverstitch is an alternative stitch that is used in lingerie, but is not always found on a home machine. Coverstitch machines can have anywhere from 2 to 4 threads. A 2 thread stitch is a chain stitch which is used in elastic attachment. 3-4 threads are used in hemming garments as well as attaching elastic around the neck and hemline of a bra.

This stitch is not as secure as a three step zigzag. If a coverstitch thread breaks on a garment, the entire stitch can fall apart.

SPECIALTY FEET ATTACHMENTS

The following feet may come in handy when sewing select elastics and fabrics.

Edge Stitching foot - This foot can be used to easily join laces and trims together. It generally has a series of guides for joining different fabric layers.

Roller foot - This foot is used in sewing knit fabrics. It helps roll the fabrics through the machine without stretching. It is not necessary to use such a foot, but it does make sewing knits much easier to handle.

NEEDLES

Dependent on the fabrics you use, you will need to choose an appropriate needle. Needles range in size and each size has a different purpose.

Smaller numbers indicate a finer needle and should be used for more delicate fabrics. Larger numbers are a thicker needle and are used for heavier fabrics.

Needles are generally labeled as 10/70 or 12/90. This indicates both the American and European size.

NEEDLE SIZES

American	European
8	60
9	65
10	70
11	75
12	80
14	90
16	100
18	110
19	120

Sharp Needles - Sharp needles are used for woven fabrics. It creates straight accurate lines of stitches.

Ballpoint Needles - Ballpoint needles are used for knits. The rounder point allows the needle to safely glide between the loops of the knit without disturbing the fibers. The stitch is not as straight as sharp needles which allows for some give on the stitch.

Universal Needles - Universal needles have many of the characteristics of both a sharp needle and a ballpoint needle. It falls in between the two. These can be used on either woven or knits, but if skipped stitches occur on a knit, opt for a ballpoint needle.

Stretch Needles - Stretch needles are recommended when sewing lycra, spandex or swimwear. This needle helps in avoiding skipped stitches.

STRETCH AND PATTERNS

Not all patterns are created equally, nor are they created for all fabrics. The patterns included in this book were designed to use two different kinds of fabrics. The front of the bra, including the cups and band, were drafted with a woven fabric without stretch. The back band was created for a power net or spandex fabric with a stretch of 50%.

To test the stretch of your fabric, fold the fabric approximately 4" or 8cm away from the cut edge of the cross grain. Place two pins 5" or 10cm apart from each other. Use the ruler on this page, placing one pin at the 0 mark and pull the fabric to its full stretched amount. Make a note of this amount. The ideal fabric to use with these patterns stretch on the cross grain 7.5" or 15cm.

These measurements are only suggestions based on how these patterns were developed. Use your own discretion in deciding on the appropriate fabric for these projects.

Centimeters
1 2 3 4 5 6 7 8 9 10 11 12 13 14 15 16 17 18 19 20 21 22

Inches
1 2 3 4 5 6 7 8 9

ELASTIC FOR PATTERNS

The elastics in a bra are used for additional support around the band and cup.

Clear Elastic - Clear elastic or Lastin can be used for reinforcement on a garment to keep the integrity of a stretch lace edge. This is generally made of Polyurethane. For the examples in the book, we use this elastic behind the edges of lace to keep the stretch stable.

Picot Edge Elastic - Picot edge elastics are available in many varieties. The picot description is of a decorative loop-type edge to an elastic. These generally come in every color under the sun. This elastic typically is in widths of 3/8" or .95cm to 5/8" or 1.6cm, although wider picot trim can be found. The elastic itself without the decorative edge is usually 1/4" or .6cm wide.

Ruffle Edge Trim - This trim is similar to the Picot edge trim but the stretch can vary from trim to trim. This trim requires careful sewing as the ruffle can easily get caught in the needle.

Strap Elastic - One side of the elastic can be brushed for comfort but the other side will always be shiny or decorative. Strap elastic can be in widths of 1/4" to 1" or .6cm to 2.5cm.

Waistband Elastic - For bra construction, you may wish to find a narrow 1/2" or 1.25cm waistband elastic. This elastic contains one side that is decorative and one side that is brushed for a soft touch to the skin. Bra waistbands and straps can be constructed from the same elastic.

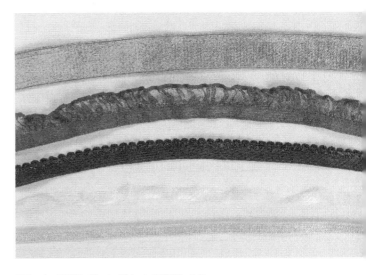

ELASTIC LENGTHS

The elastic on bras is treated differently than on panties and other lingerie. The elastic lengths can sometimes be stretched, but mostly, the elastics are the exact length of the finished garment.

To determine the length of elastic needed for your bra, measure each portion. Where a single piece of elastic spans more than one pattern piece, subtract the seam allowance in between.

Use the illustration below as a guide for filling out the neckline measurements on the following page.

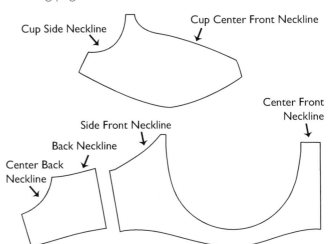

Cup Side Neckline

Cup Center Front Neckline

Center Front Neckline

Side Front Neckline

Back Neckline

Center Back Neckline

NECKLINE MEASUREMENTS	
Center Front Neckline	
Cup Center Front Neckline	
Side Cup Neckline	
Side Front Neckline	
Back Neckline	
Subtract 1" or 2.5cm	
Center Back Neckline	

BRA MEASUREMENTS

In the back of this book, I have provided a basic full coverage bra pattern for your use. These patterns are to act as a teaching aid in learning basic sewing of bras and making pattern alterations. These patterns were created from the drafting and grading instructions in the Advanced section of this book.

The basic patterns included in this book consist of two piece cup. Please note that a two piece cup may not be ideal for bust diameters over 8". In Chapter 3, we alter a basic two piece cup into multiple pieces which is more conducive for larger bust diameters.

WHY IS IT SO HARD TO FIND A BRA THAT FITS RIGHT?

Nearly every woman has been measured for a bra at least once in her life. It is a somewhat frustrating process in which 80% of the time, the bra fitter places the individual in the wrong size. In my quest of writing this book, I ventured out to answer why that is.

My conclusions determine that incorrect bra fitting happens for these two main reasons:

1. *Measurements are being taken without knowing how they relate to the number on the bra*

2. *Measurements are being taken on women who are already wearing the wrong size bra.*

To address the first reason, answer this question: What do the numbers mean on your bra? The numbers on your bra have different meanings in different countries.

In France, the number on the bra indicates the measurement of your chest above the breast tissue.

In Europe and other international countries (not including the UK), the number on the bra indicates the measurement taken directly below the bust on the rib cage.

Italian and Australian bra sizes don't have any relationship to either of these measurements, just international sizes in general.

That just leaves the US and UK sizing. US/UK sizing is not as simple as French or international sizing, but it does relate to both of those measurements. US/UK sizing is based on the average between the two measurements. The next page has a basic conversion chart to show band size conversion for different countries.

BAND SIZE CONVERSION

US/UK	Europe/ International	France	Italy	Australia
28				
30	65	80	0	8
32	70	85	1	10
34	75	90	2	12
36	80	95	3	14
38	85	100	4	16
40	90	105	5	18
42	95	110	6	20
44	100	115		
46	105	120		
48	110	125		
50	105	130		

To address the second issue; many bra fitters take measurements to determine the cup size by measuring the bust circumference. This is usually not very accurate as most women are not wearing the correct size bra in the first place.

This number is not reliable, as it depends on where the breast is sitting. If the bust sags due to age or bra size, the circumference will vary and so will the cup size.

TAKING MEASUREMENTS

To take proper measurements, one should do so without wearing a bra. If measuring yourself, you may wish to take these measurements without any undergarments on. If you are measuring someone else, have them wear a tank top or a snug fitting tee shirt.

If taking your own measurements, set aside all preconceived notions of what bra you may normally wear, and take the measurements needing for drafting a custom bra. You will need some string or ribbon to tie around your model or yourself, a tape measure and a full length mirror.

Take the tape measure and measure the chest measurement and the under bust measurement. These should be snug measurements.

The second part requires one to measure the diameter of the bust from the chest to the under bust. To get your bust measurement, tie one length of string around the chest above the breast tissue. Tie another length of string around the rib cage directly below the breast.

If taking your own measurements, look in the mirror, line the tape measure at the tie below your bust and stretch it directly over your apex up to the top tie, keeping the tape measure perpendicular to the two ties. This will indicate the bust diameter.

One thing to consider is that most women are not the same size on both breasts. Measure both for accuracy. Record your measurements on the following chart.

Chest Measurement	
Under Bust Measurement	
Left Bust Diameter	
Right Bust Diameter	

To determine the cup size, there is some complexity to it. Cup size has two factors in play, body circumference and bust diameter.

The patterns provided in the back of this book use the size charts below. This chart represents the US/UK standard, in which the band size is determined as the average of the chest and under bust measurements. Add the two measurements together and divide by 2 to achieve the average. Round to the nearest whole even number.

| Chest Measurement |
| Under Bust Measurement |
| Average (Band Size) |

Please note that there is no standard size chart that all manufacturers use. Your bra size may vary based on manufacturer, but you can use

BRA CUP SIZE - IMPERIAL
Measurements in Inches

Band Size	Bust Diameter														
	3.5	4	4.5	5	5.5	6	6.5	7	7.5	8	8.5	9	9.5	10	10.5
28	A	B	C	D	E	F	G	H	I	J	K	L			
30		AA	A	B	C	D	E	F	G	H	I	J	K	L	
32			AAA	AA	A	B	C	D	E	F	G	H	I	J	K
34					AAA	AA	A	B	C	D	E	F	G	H	I
36							AAA	AA	A	B	C	D	E	F	G
38									AAA	AA	A	B	C	D	E
40											AAA	AA	A	B	C
42													AAA	AA	A
44															AAA

Band Size	Bust Diameter														
	11	11.5	12	12.5	13	13.5	14	14.5	15	15.5	16	16.5	17	17.5	18
32	L														
34	J	K	L												
36	H	I	J	K	L										
38	F	G	H	I	J	K	L								
40	D	E	F	G	H	I	J	K	L						
42	B	C	D	E	F	G	H	I	J	K	L				
44	AA	A	B	C	D	E	F	G	H	I	J	K	L		
46		AAA	AA	A	B	C	D	E	F	G	H	I	J	K	
48				AAA	AA	A	B	C	D	E	F	G	H	I	J
50						AAA	AA	A	B	C	D	E	F	G	H

this chart as a starting point when determining what size you wear in ready-to-wear brands.

This book contains sizes 30A to 40F. Additional sizes from 30G through 40J are available online at www.losangelesfashionresource.com. For larger sizes, custom bra drafting directions are found in the Advanced section.

It is my recommendation that AA and AAA use the same band as A and all cups over J use the same band size as J. This is suggested because of wire sizes. Larger wires may dig into the underarm and smaller wires may be too small for the body frame.

BRA CUP SIZE - METRIC
Measurements in Centimeters

Band Size	Bust Diameter														
	8.75	10	11.25	12.5	13.75	15	16.25	17.5	18.75	20	21.25	22.5	23.75	25	26.25
28	A	B	C	D	E	F	G	H	I	J	K	L			
30		AA	A	B	C	D	E	F	G	H	I	J	K	L	
32			AAA	AA	A	B	C	D	E	F	G	H	I	J	K
34					AAA	AA	A	B	C	D	E	F	G	H	I
36							AAA	AA	A	B	C	D	E	F	G
38								AAA	AA	A	B	C	D	E
40										AAA	AA	A	B	C
42												AAA	AA	A
44															AAA

Band Size	Bust Diameter														
	27.5	28.75	30	31.25	32.5	33.75	35	36.25	37.5	38.75	40	41.25	42.5	43.75	45
32	L														
34	J	K	L												
36	H	I	J	K	L										
38	F	G	H	I	J	K	L								
40	D	E	F	G	H	I	J	K	L						
42	B	C	D	E	F	G	H	I	J	K	L				
44	AA	A	B	C	D	E	F	G	H	I	J	K	L		
46		AAA	AA	A	B	C	D	E	F	G	H	I	J	K	
48				AAA	AA	A	B	C	D	E	F	G	H	I	J
50						AAA	AA	A	B	C	D	E	F	G	H

SELECTING UNDERWIRES

Once a band and cup size has been determined, an underwire size must be selected. The underwire is related to the chart we used to determine the cup size. One underwire can fit up to 10 different sizes depending on the measurements. US/UK underwires are generally sized by even numbers 28-60. Australian, Italian, French and international wires are based on the size conversion chart on page 21.

The underwires used in this book are full underwires. To fit a wire to the body, place it

IMPERIAL WIRE CHART

Band Size	Bust Diameter														
	3.5	4	4.5	5	5.5	6	6.5	7	7.5	8	8.5	9	9.5	10	10.5
28	28	30	32	34	36	38	40	42	44						
30		28	30	32	34	36	38	40	42	44	46				
32			28	30	32	34	36	38	40	42	44	46	48		
34					30	32	34	36	38	40	42	44	46	48	50
36							32	34	36	38	40	42	44	46	48
38									34	36	38	40	42	44	46
40											36	38	40	42	44
42													38	40	42
44															40

Band Size	Bust Diameter														
	11	11.5	12	12.5	13	13.5	14	14.5	15	15.5	16	16.5	17	17.5	18
36	50	52													
38	48	50	52	54											
40	46	48	50	52	54	56									
42	44	46	48	50	52	54	56	58							
44	42	44	46	48	50	52	54	56	58	60					
46		42	44	46	48	50	52	54	56	58	60				
48				44	46	48	50	52	54	56	58	60			
50					46	48	50	52	54	56	58	60			

under and around the bust. A properly fitting underwire will encase all or most of the breast tissue.

Referring to the band size and bust diameter, choose the most appropriate underwire size.

When fitting an underwire, note comfort levels as the wire size increases and where it ends under the arm. On occasion, a wire that fits the breast tissue will sometimes dig into the underarm. If this is the case, use the next smaller underwire or cut the wire height down to size.

METRIC WIRE CHART

Band Size	Bust Diameter														
	8.75	10	11.25	12.5	13.75	15	16.25	17.5	18.75	20	21.25	22.5	23.75	25	26.25
28	28	30	32	34	36	38	40	42	44						
30		28	30	32	34	36	38	40	42	44	46				
32			28	30	32	34	36	38	40	42	44	46	48		
34					30	32	34	36	38	40	42	44	46	48	50
36							32	34	36	38	40	42	44	46	48
38									34	36	38	40	42	44	46
40											36	38	40	42	44
42													38	40	42
44															40

Band Size	Bust Diameter														
	27.5	28.75	30	31.25	32.5	33.75	35	36.25	37.5	38.75	40	41.25	42.5	43.75	45
36	50	52													
38	48	50	52	54											
40	46	48	50	52	54	56									
42	44	46	48	50	52	54	56	58							
44	42	44	46	48	50	52	54	56	58	60					
46		42	44	46	48	50	52	54	56	58	60				
48				44	46	48	50	52	54	56	58	60			
50						46	48	50	52	54	56	58	60		

UNDERSTANDING FIT

The fit of a bra can be a challenging thing to identify since so many people are regularly wearing the incorrect size. The following list will help you identify a bad fit.

1. **The back of the band is yanked up high.** If the band is not level around the body and is lifted higher in the back, your band is either too big or your straps are too tight.

2. **The straps are digging into the shoulder leaving an indentation in the shoulder.** This is usually due to the band and cup fitting incorrectly. 90% of a bra should be supported by the band. If your straps dig in, loosen the straps to their fullest and see what the bra does.

3. **The band is not sitting flush to the skin.** The band is support to hold up the cups and is supposed to be snug on the body. If the wearer lifts their arms and the band moves the band is too big or the cups are too small. Just the same, if you can place a finger under the band at the center front, the bra has similar issues.

4. **The breast tissue is dented and overflows where the cup lies across the body.** This is especially visible in a snug tee shirt. This indicates that the cup is too small.

5. **The underwire is digging into the underarm.** The band is too big for the body. The underwire should sit next to the breast tissue, not in the underarm.

6. **Back fat bulging from under the band in the back or side seam.** This could either be a band that is too small or a band that is too big. A properly fitting bra should comfortably contain your "extra" skin.

The first step to a properly fitting bra is to get the correct band, then to fit the bust. Start with a larger cup size to ensure that the band fits the body snug and in the correct place.

CHAPTER 2

BASIC BRA CONSTRUCTION

There are many methods to construct a bra, this chapter introduces one of them. The following chapters introduce alternative methods. For this example, we will construct the bra that is provided in the back of the book. This design will have a simple 1/2" or 1.25cm picot elastic trim applied to the neckline and waistline.

In preparation, cut two top and bottom cups, one center front band on the fold and two side front bands out of your woven design fabric. Cut two back bands from power net. Cut two side front bands and one center front band on the fold from a stabilizer. Use the following chart to record your measurements to determine the elastic measurements.

Center Front Cup Neckline		Center Back Neckline	
Side Cup Neckline		Center Front Waistline	
Side Front Neckline		Side Front Waistline	
Back Neckline		Back Waistline	
Subtract 1" or 2.5cm		Subtract 1" or 2.5cm	

CUP CONSTRUCTION

1. With the right sides facing each other, place the cup pieces together.

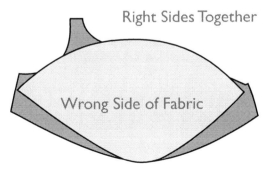

Right Sides Together

Wrong Side of Fabric

2. Pin the edges together and stitch together at 1/4" or .6cm with a straight stitch. This will require slight manipulation of the fabrics to line up the curved edges.

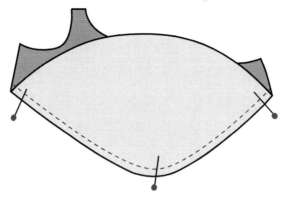

3. Open the cup and press the seam open.

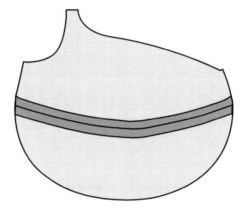

4. Trim down the seam allowance to 1/8" or .3cm. Place a shear strip of seam tape over the seam allowance and pin in place. For first time construction, you may wish to loosely hand baste in place.

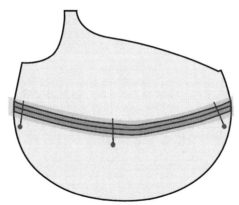

5. Sew two rows of stitching on both sides of the seam securing the seam tape over the seam allowance.

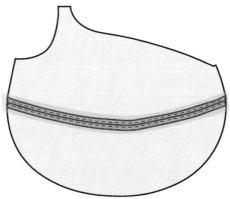

6. Before continuing to the remainder of the bra, picot elastic needs to be attached to the center neckline of the cup.

    a. Place the decorative side of the elastic toward the right side of the fabric and stitch in place closely and evenly to the picot edge. This can be done with an overlock, zigzag or straight stitch. Do not stretch the fabric when sewing.

    TIP: if you are using the overlock machine, make sure not to cut the elastic. Cutting the elastic causes the elastic to lose its stability. This can result in the elastic stretching out rapidly.

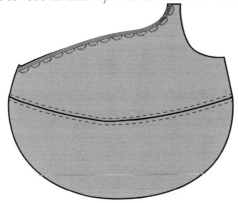

    b. Flip the elastic so the stitched side appears on the back side of the garment and the decorative edge is the only part visible on the right side of the garment.

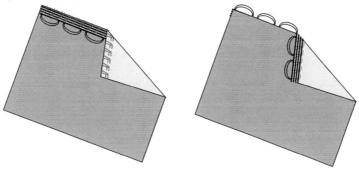

7. With the elastic flipped, stitch in place with either a zigzag or three step zigzag stitch.

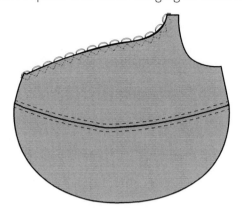

BAND CONSTRUCTION

8. On the center front, place the stabilizer and center band piece with right sides together (or the soft side of the stabilizer inwards) and stitch the neckline portion at 1/4" or .6cm with a straight stitch.

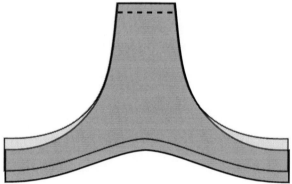

9. Flip the stabilizer to the backside of the band and secure in place by stitching around all the edges at 1/8" or .3cm. If you are an experienced sewer, you can stitch down the neckline portion and pin the remainder securely, although this may be tricky with attaching the cup and elastics.

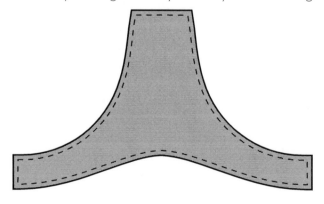

10. On the side front band, place the stabilizer behind the band with wrong side of the stabilizer facing the wrong side of the band. Stitch in place at 1/8" or .3cm.

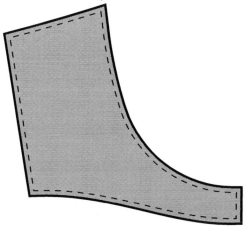

11. Connect the center front band to the side front band with right sides together at 1/4" or .6cm. Press the seams open.

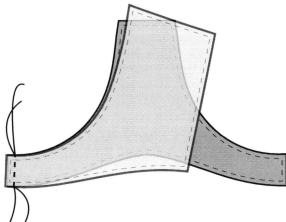

12. Attach the front band to the back band at the side seam with a straight stitch at 1/4" or .6cm and press towards the front.

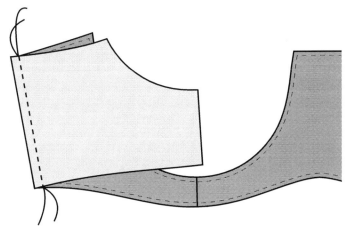

13. For added support on larger cups and bands, boning can be added to the side seam.

    a. Measure the side seam from top to bottom. Remove 1/2" or 1.25cm from the distance and cut this amount of casing. The boning should be about 1/4" or .6cm smaller than the casing length.

Side Seam	
Subtract 1/2" or 1.25cm	
Casing Size	
Subtract 1/4" or .6cm	
Boning Size	

    b. Attach the casing edge to the seam allowance on the back side of the band, leaving 1/4" or .6cm at both the top and bottom.

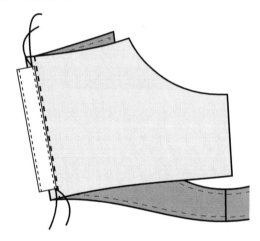

    c. Fold the casing flat towards the front side of the band and top stitch the remaining side in place stitching from the top edge of the band to the bottom.

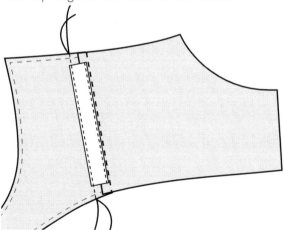

14. Place and stitch the waistband elastic around the waistline with the decorative side facing the right side of the fabric.

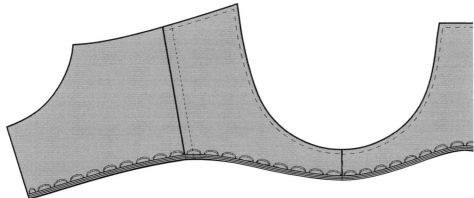

15. Fold the elastic to the backside and secure with a zigzag or three step zigzag stitch.

16. Attach the cup into the curve of the band with right sides facing each other. If this is your first time sewing a bra, I would recommend hand basting these pieces in place prior to sewing by machine. Stitch in place with a straight stitch at 1/4" or .6cm.

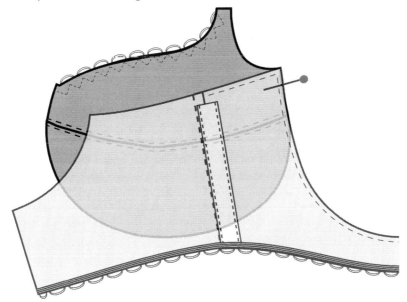

17. Measure the seam line stitched in #16. Subtract 1/4" or .6cm from the length. Cut this length in underwire channeling. We reduce it by 1/4" or .6cm for applying the neckline elastic under the arm.

Cup Seam Length	
Subtract 1/4" or .62cm	
Channeling Length	

18. Take the underwire channeling and attach it to the seam allowance on the cup side as we did for the boning casing. Begin from the underarm 1/4" or .6cm away from the end and stitch it all the way to the center front neckline. This should end at the center front neckline. Trim it to fit.

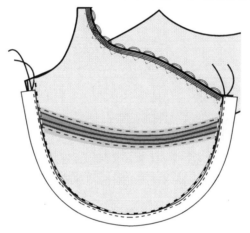

19. Fold the channeling towards the band and top stitch the remaining side in place.

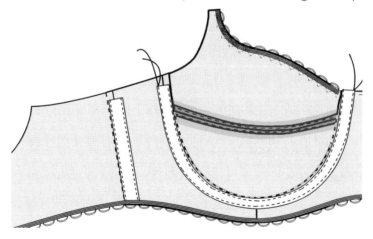

20. Attach the neckline elastic from the strap point to the top of the cup.

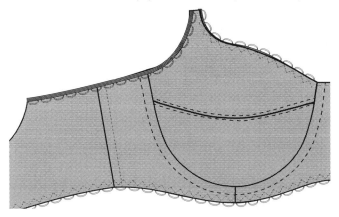

21. a. Insert the boning into the casing at the side seam.

   b. Flip the elastic to the backside of the bra and top stitch with a zigzag. Be careful, stitching through the boning is possible. As long as the boning is plastic, stitch slowly and it should not break the needle.

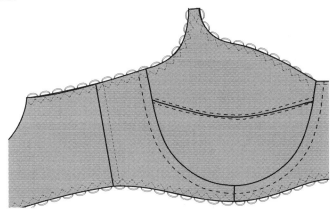

22. Add 1/2" or 1.25cm to your center back elastic measurement. On the back band of the bra, attach the center back elastic. Leave the additional 1/2" or 1.25cm of elastic at the strap point.

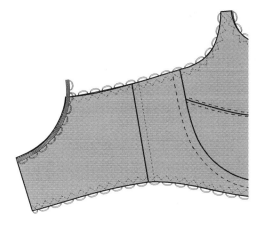

23. To construct a strap one will need strap elastic, a slider and a ring.

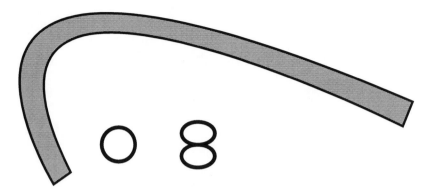

24. Loop the elastic through the center of the slider and secure in place with a bar tack or a shallow and small zigzag stitch.

25. Place the elastic through the ring and pass the elastic through the slider a second time.

26. Attach the strap end to the front neckline with the right sides facing each other.

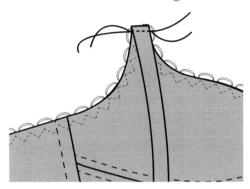

27. Flip the strap to show the right side and bar tack in place, securing the strap and cup seam allowance down.

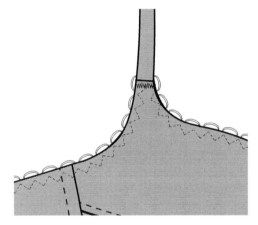

28. Attach the ring of your strap to the elastic at the back strap point by passing the picot end through the ring and securing it to the back side of the band. Bar tack in place.

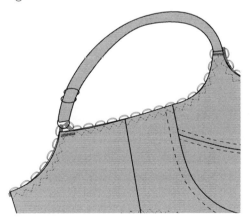

29. Insert the underwire into the channeling at the center front of the bra. Bar tack the end of the casing to the band at center front.

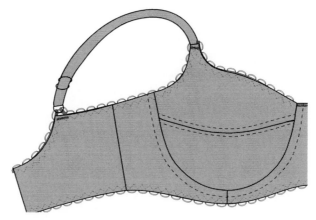

30. Hook & eye tape usually has an open flap for placing over the end of the bra backs.

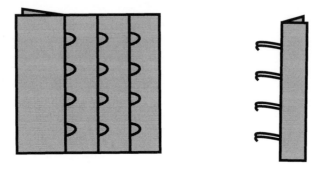

31. Use a zipper foot to baste the tape in place. Use a regular foot or an adjustable zipper foot to zigzag over the edge to clean finish the flap. Attach the hooks on the left side of the bra and the eyes on the right side of the bra back.

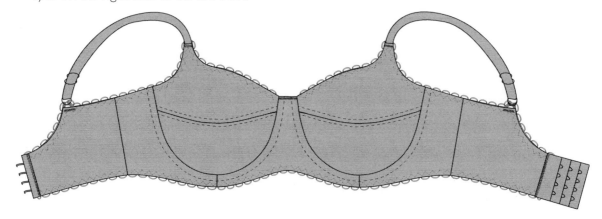

CHAPTER 3

BASIC BRA WITH MULTI-SEAMED CUP.

This chapter introduces pattern manipulation by changing the two piece cup into a three piece cup. This chapter also utilizes a 3/4" or 1.9cm elastic for the waistline and center back neckline, a 1/2" or 1.25cm picot elastic for the center and side neckline, and a fully lined cup.

PART 1: PATTERN MANIPULATION

1. Trace the lower bra cup.

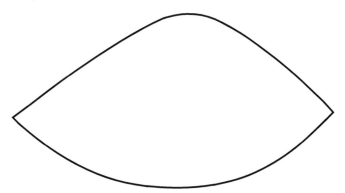

2. Cut the lower cup into two pieces. Choose a seam line of your preference.

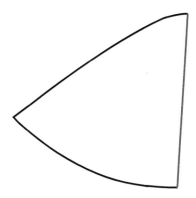 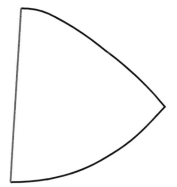

3. To achieve a better fit, a curve needs to be added to the straight line. Use the following curve extension chart based on the diameter of the cup. The following table is a suggested guideline for determining the amount of curve that is needed.

IMPERIAL MEASUREMENTS
Measurements in Inches

Diameter	Amount	Diameter	Amount
5	1/8	12	5/16
5 1/2	1/8	12 1/2	5/16
6	1/8	13	5/16
6 1/2	3/16	13 1/2	5/16
7	3/16	14	3/8
7 1/2	3/16	14 1/2	3/8
8	3/16	15	3/8
8 1/2	3/16	15 1/2	3/8
9	1/4	16	3/8
9 1/2	1/4	16 1/2	7/16
10	1/4	17	7/16
10 1/2	1/4	17 1/2	7/16
11	1/4	18	7/16
11 1/2	5/16		

METRIC MEASUREMENTS
Measurements in Centimeters

Diameter	Amount	Diameter	Amount
12.5	0.3	30	0.8
13.75	0.3	31.25	0.8
15	0.4	32.5	0.8
16.25	0.4	33.75	0.8
17.5	0.4	35	0.9
18.75	0.5	36.25	0.9
20	0.5	37.5	0.9
21.25	0.5	38.75	1.0
22.5	0.6	40	1.0
23.75	0.6	41.25	1.0
25	0.6	42.5	1.1
26.25	0.7	43.75	1.1
27.5	0.7	45	1.1
28.75	0.7		

Use the following chart to record your measurements and the amount of the curve extension.

Left Bust Diameter		Amount	
Right Bust Diameter		Amount	

4. At the half way point on the straight line mark out the amount defined above.

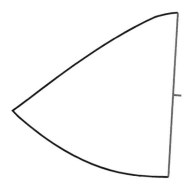 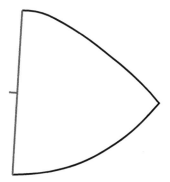

5. Take your hip curve and connect the lower point, the half way point and the tip. Place the curved part of the ruler closer to the tip.

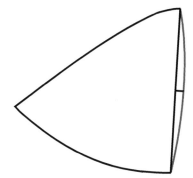 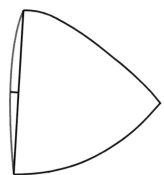

6. Add 1/4" or .6cm seam allowance to the curves.

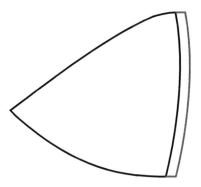 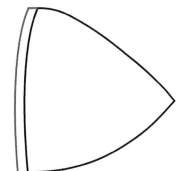

7. Trace the band pattern pieces. Draw in the seam allowances on the front joining seams as pictured.

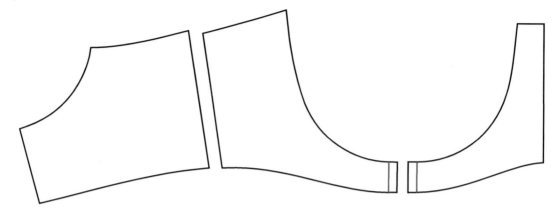

8. Overlap the front band pieces at the seam lines. These pattern pieces will be joined for this pattern. The front band is sometimes split in two pieces to conserve fabric. Keeping a full front piece is a more expensive method to construct the band.

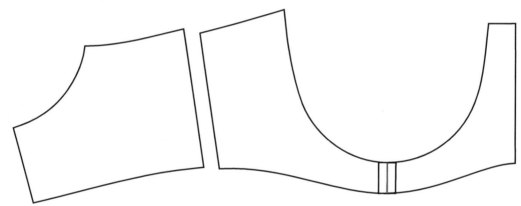

9. Remove 1/4" or .6cm off the waistline of the band. The elastic will be attached in a different method and in order to attach it in this manner and still have it fit with hook & eyes, we must alter the waistline depth.

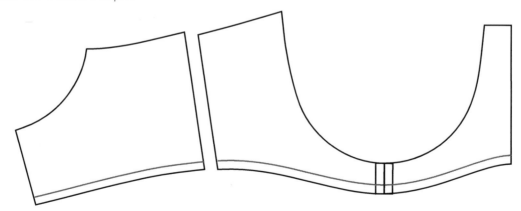

10. Remove 3/4" or 1.9cm off the back neckline from the center back to the back strap.

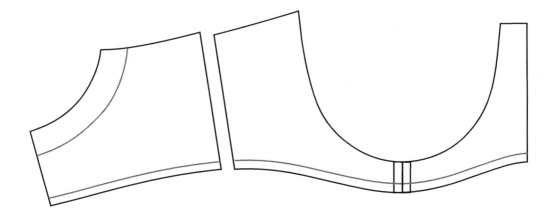

PART 2: CONSTRUCTION METHOD

This section introduces a new method to attach elastic to the waistline and adds an attached back strap to the back neckline. These directions also introduce a fully lined cup. A lined cup is used when the design fabric has too much stretch or if it might cause irritation to the skin.

I. Cut out two sets of patterns for the cup. One of the design fabric and one of a softer breathable fabric for the lining. A tricot is a great fabric to use for such a lining.

Design Fabric   Lining Fabric

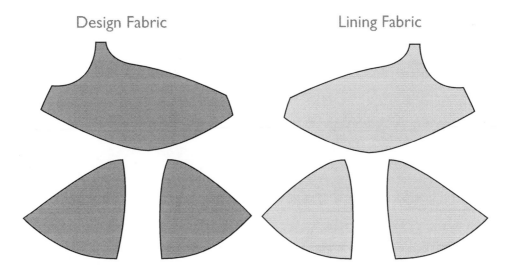

2. Attach the two lower cups together at 1/4" or .6cm of both the lining and the design fabric.

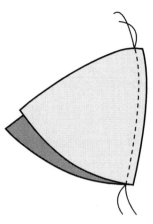

3. Press the seams open and top stitch the seams down close to the seam. You may trim down the seam allowance to 1/8" or .3cm to reduce bulk.

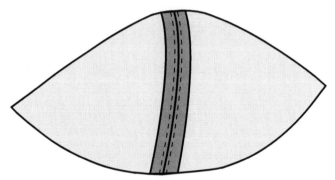

4. Sew the lower cup to the upper cup at 1/4" or .6cm. Press open and top stitch.

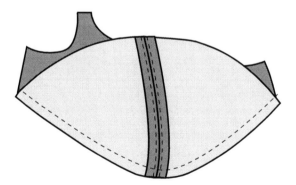

5. Take the right side of the design fabric cup and place your decorative elastic at the center neckline of the cup. Baste stitch in place.

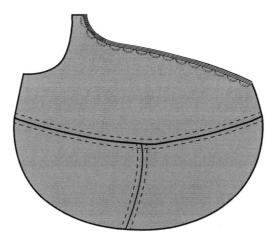

6. Place the right side of the lining towards the right side of the design fabric. Sew the neckline together at 1/4" or .6cm, sandwiching the elastic in between the two layers. At the center front of the neckline, stop sewing 1/4" or .6cm away from the end (this will aid in attaching the cup to the band).

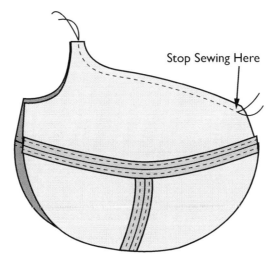

Stop Sewing Here

7. Flip right sides out and stitch the edges together to hold the two layers in place.

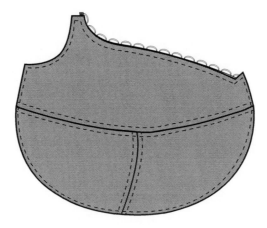

Continue with steps 8 through 13 from Chapter 2, then complete with the following steps.

14. Instead of attaching the elastic at the waistline as demonstrated in Chapter 2, overlap the elastic on top of the raw edge by 1/4" or .6cm. Use a 3/4" or 1.9cm elastic.

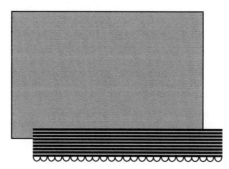

Stitch in place with a zigzag or coverstitch. A coverstitch is ideal for this finishing because it covers the raw edge underneath with a covered stitch.

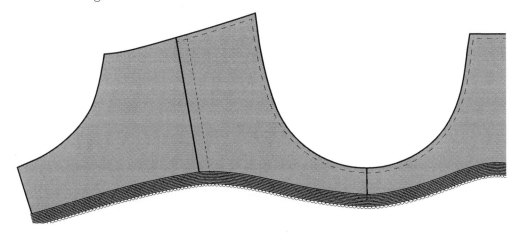

Continue with steps 15 through 20 from Chapter 2.

21. Cut a length of elastic that will expand the back neckline and become the strap. A standard strap measures between 15" and 18" or 38cm to 45cm.

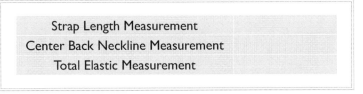

Strap Length Measurement	
Center Back Neckline Measurement	
Total Elastic Measurement	

22. Overlap the back neckline with the elastic by 1/4" or .6cm as we did for the waistline. Attach the elastic and secure at the top of the back band with a bar tack.

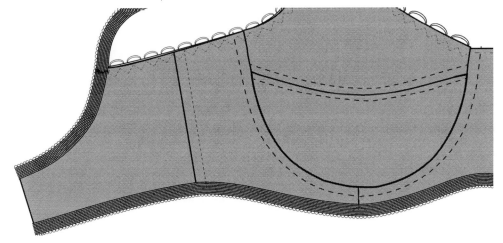

23. Add the slider and ring to the end of the strap. Attach the ring to the front of the bra by looping the strap point through the ring. Bar tack in place.

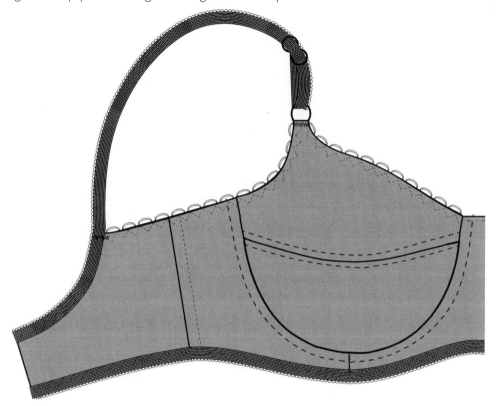

To complete this bra, follow steps 30 and 31 from Chapter 2. The hook and eye will be one row larger due to the change we made at the waistline and back neck.

CHAPTER 4
BRA BAND WITH FLOATING CUPS

Some bra designs have only a partial band, meaning that the band itself is segmented on the sides of the cup. This chapter alters the basic bra pattern to create a bra with floating cups, where the band is not attached to the entire cup. For a construction variation, the cup center neckline will use a decorative edge lace fabric and a variation for attaching straps.

PART 1: PATTERN MANIPULATION

1. Trace the cup patterns.

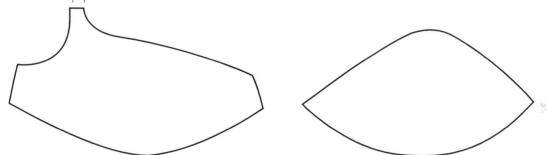

2. The first change will be to alter the neckline for a straight edge lace. Draw a straight line from the right side of the strap to the center front neckline. You will use this neckline as the edge of the lace. Because of this change, the grainline will differ and alterations to fit properly may be needed.

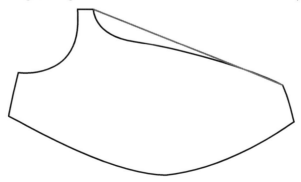

3. Normally the underwire channeling is folded outwards and stitched down to the band. Because this bra does not have a full band, the channeling must be sewn to the cup instead. As to not lose any volume of the cup, we need to add the amount we will lose due to the underwire attachment.

At the curve, where it is sewn to the band, add 1/2" or 1.25cm (the approximate width of the underwire channeling). Due to the change at the center front. Revise the neckline to a straight line again.

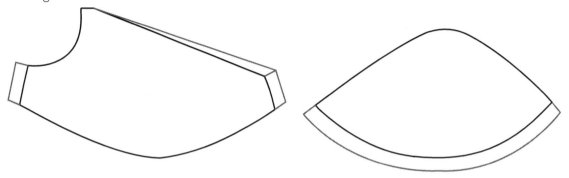

4. Trace all the band pieces and draw in the seam allowances at the side seam and center cup at 1/4" or .6cm.

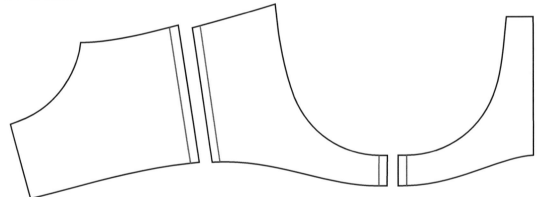

5. Connect the back band to the side front band by overlapping them at the seam allowances. Connect the center band to the side band in the same manner. Do not remove the seam allowances; they will be separated in a few steps.

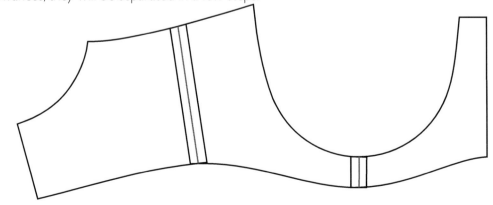

6. Keeping the top of the center front panel, adjust the band shape removing a portion of the lower band. Alter the side band to your preference by removing the lower front connecting band. In this example, I am removing the back strap curve.

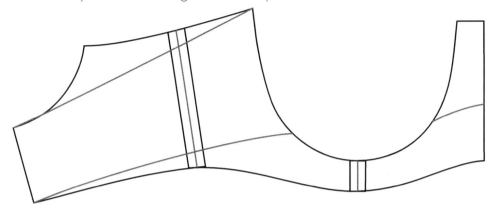

7. Separate the three pattern pieces. All seam allowances should be included, providing you did not remove them in step 5.

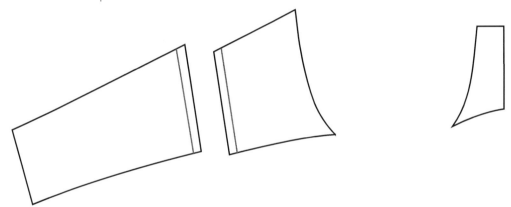

8. Because volume was added to the cup, the band needs to be altered to balance that amount. Remove 1/2" or 1.25cm from the band where the cup is inserted.

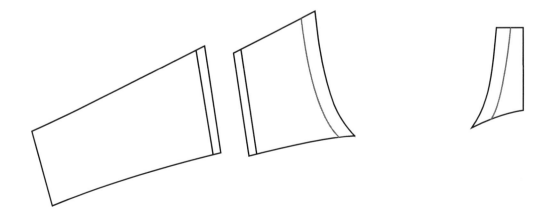

PART 2: CONSTRUCTION METHOD

Using a lace with a finished edge, line up the top front neckline to the edge of the fabric and cut out your piece.

CUP CONSTRUCTION

5. Attach the cup seams together as shown in Chapter 2, steps 1 through 5.

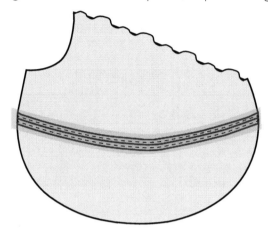

6. Due to the nature of lace, the edge needs to be reinforced by either clear elastic or seam tape. Both serve the purpose of securing the neckline.

    a. The elastic can be stitched in with a zigzag, slightly stretched to hug the neckline. **OR**

    b. The seam tape can be stitched, with a straight stitch, to secure the fabric from stretching.

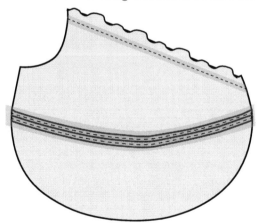

BAND CONSTRUCTION

7. Place the right side of the bridge to the right side of the stabilizer. Stitch the tops and bottoms together at 1/4" or .6cm.

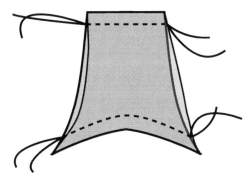

8. Flip right sides out and stitch around the edges at 1/8" or .3cm.

Complete steps 12 through 15 from Chapter 2.

For the side front band, stitch the stabilizer to the band. Continue by attaching the side seams, boning casing and the waistband elastic.

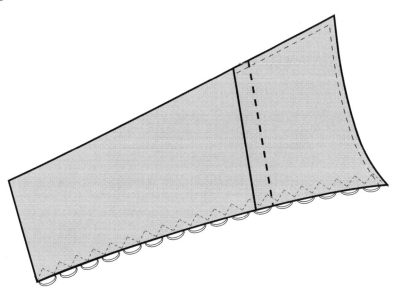

16. Beginning at the top of the cup by the center front, attach the bridge to the cup at 1/4" or .6cm.

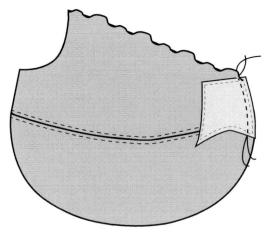

17. Attach the top of the side cup to the band at 1/4" or .6cm.

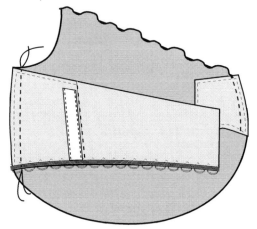

18. Measure the distance around the cup curve at the seam line (1/4" or .6cm from the cup edge). Remove 1/4" or .6cm for spacing at the underarm elastic. Cut a piece of underwire channeling for this amount. This amount will differ from Chapter 2 due to changes to the cup size.

Cup Seam Measurement	
Subtract 1/4"	
Channeling Length	

19. Take the underwire channeling and attach it to the seam allowance of the cup curve just short of 1/4" or .6cm. Instead of attaching it to the wrong side of the cup as we did in Chapter 2, attach it to the right side of the cup on the seam line. Start 1/4" or .6cm down from the side cup. The channeling should end at the center front neckline, if it extends past, trim down.

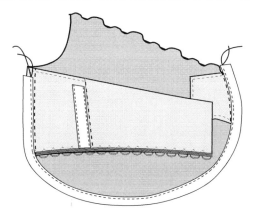

20. Fold the channeling inwards to the cup and top stitch the edge in place.

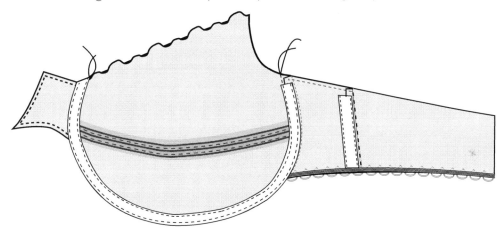

21. Attach picot elastic to the neckline of the back and side cup.

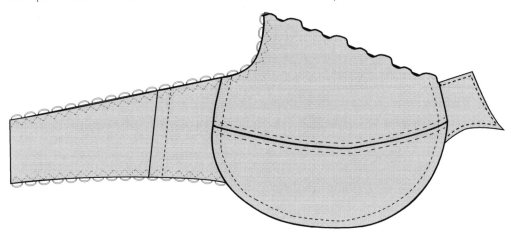

22. For the styling of this back band, it is recommended to use a reinforced strap or "T" strap. Take the strap with an "O" ring at the end. At the bottom of the "O" ring, loop a length of elastic equal to twice the back band height. This strap will be attached at the top and bottom of the band.

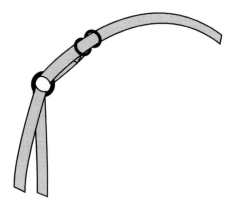

23. At the strap position or middle of the back band, attach the bottom of the elastic to the bottom of the band with a bar tack. Reinforce the top of the elastic at the top of the band with another bar tack.

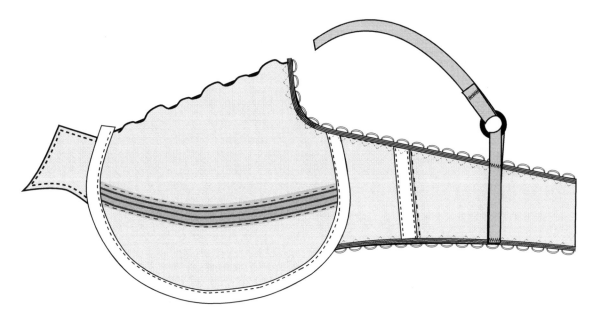

For completion of this bra, follow steps 26, 27, 30 and 31 from Chapter 2.

INTERMEDIATE

CHAPTER 5

INTRODUCTION TO PATTERN MANIPULATION

The Intermediate section highlights how to perform pattern alterations, including adding style lines and creating specialty bras. These include soft bras, nursing bras, mastectomy bras and strapless bras.

TOOLS

Awl - An awl is a pointed tool that resembles an ice pick. It is used for making drill holes or indicator holes in garment construction to mark boning, darts and pocket placement.

Notcher - A notcher is a small handheld device that places small cutouts on the edge of your patterns. It looks like a hole punch, but costs a pretty penny.

Select notching should be done on patterns to indicate stitch lines. Excessive notching on garments with small seam allowances is ill advised.

Notches can be placed outwards as a "V," as seen on manufactured patterns or inwards using a notcher.

Pinpoint Tracing Wheel - Much like the tracing wheel found in traditional fabric stores, this wheel contains spikes to transfer markings from one layer of paper to another.

Pintucking Foot - As opposed to manually pintucking fabric by folding and stitching, this foot guides the fabric evenly through the sewing machine and evenly spaces the pintucks.

Wire Cutters - A small pair of wire cutters or pliers with wire cutting capabilities are recommended to alter wire lengths for custom or demi wires.

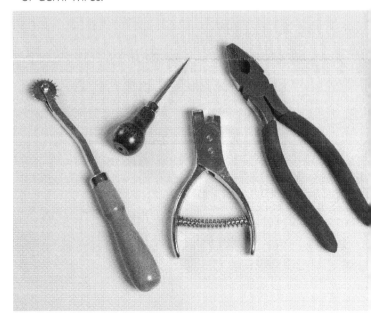

SUPPLIES

Some of these specialty supplies can be found at your local fabric and craft store. For others, bra construction suppliers will need to be your source. A small variety of these are available on our publisher's website.

Batting - Batting or foam is used to pad a cup. Different weights and concentrations are available in widths of 1/8" to 1/2". Batting can be cotton, poly-cotton or 100% poly-fill.

Front Clip - Front clips are generally plastic and allow for an easy open and close functionality to a bra. The disadvantage: a front closure does not allow a bra to adjust in size as a hook and eye closure allows.

Gripper Elastic - Gripper elastics contain a narrow strip of rubber on the back side. Gripper elastics can be used for strapless bras, bustiers and shape wear.

Nursing Clip - A nursing clip is a specialty clip which allows a nursing mother to open and close her nursing cup with one hand. An alternative to this is to use a slide hook.

Separator - Separators are heavy gauge wires that are used in the center of cups for plunge shapes on bras or bustiers. They are often referred to as U-wires or V-wires, which are defined by their shape.

Slide Hook - A slide hook can range in size from 1/4" to 1". This type of hook is used in swimwear and used for nursing bra cup access. These can be in metal or plastic form. Slide

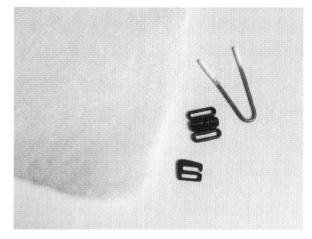

hooks look like a slider, but one side remains open for hooking to a fabric loop.

BASIC ALTERATIONS

The alterations discussed in this section are basic and simple changes. I encourage you to experiment with your own styles. Be sure to test each design for fit and functionality. Every pattern change affects the fit of a garment; where the bra sits on the body and how it covers the bust.

SOFT BRA

A non-wired bra is often called a soft bra. This style of bra is generally seen with cups A-C as they don't need the support of an underwire, although larger cupped soft bras are available.

Soft bras have a variety of different styles. The directions in this book alter the cup and band shapes. A wire supports the bust, to achieve a similar support one must give the breast more support on the band and at the neckline.

Some individuals may use the same patterns as an underwire bra. The difference is in construction. Underwire channeling is used with the exclusion of adding the underwire. This method will offer support, but may not be ideal for larger cup sizes.

NURSING BRA

Nursing bras are unique in that they require a cup to partially detach while remaining fully supportive. A nursing bra can be adapted from either a wired or a non-wired bra style.

If a nursing mother chooses to wear an underwire bra, it is even more important that the bra fits properly. If the wire does not sit properly under the breast, it can restrict the mammary glands and cause mastitis, a major health issue for nursing women.

MASTECTOMY BRA

Mastectomy bras are usually traditional bras that are altered to add a pocket for a prosthetic. Mastectomy bras can also be underwire or non-wired, although the absence of underwire is more conducive to supporting certain prosthetics.

Prosthetics are available in a variety of shapes and sizes depending on the manufacturer and needs of the customer. When developing a mastectomy bra, it is crucial that you know the shape and size of the prosthetic being used.

PADDING

The chapter on padding details how to create a foam insert as well how to create a seamed and padded cup.

An alternative is to purchase a manufactured molded and/or padded cup. This type of padding is regularly found in ready-to-wear. These can be custom made to your specifications, but creating molds can be costly depending on the range of sizes you wish to produce.

DEMI CUP BRA

A demi bra is a 3/4 coverage bra that dips low in the front. This type of bra is used to enhance the bust and is generally designed for smaller cup sizes. Because the front dips low, this style bra is ideal for a front hook closure. The downside to a front hook closure is the lack of adjustability when bra elastic stretches out of shape.

Demi underwires are generally about 1-1/2" or 3.8cm shorter than a full coverage wire at the center front. Demi wires can be cut down from a full wire. This allows for more versatility in a custom design.

Related to the demi cup is the semi cup and quarter cup. A semi cup is a half cup that generally cuts across the apex. A quarter cup is a bra that contains only half of a lower cup and does not cover the apex.

STRAPLESS BRA

The strapless bra varies from the basic bra in that the band is more supportive and covers more of the body. A strapless bra generally has boning and a wider hook & eye closure. There are a variety of strapless designs including backless and plunge.

Backless bras are not entirely backless, but have a long base so a garment with a low cut back will not show the bra. This type of bra will have more boning than an average strapless bra and looks like a bustier or corset.

For backless strapless bra designs, a few additional measurements are needed for development. Similar to measurements taken in the Beginner section, take 2 ribbons and tie one below the bust and one at the natural waistline. The natural waistline is the narrowest point of the body, generally several inches above the navel.

Take the measurement of the waistline and the measurement of the distance from the under bust ribbon to the waistline ribbon.

Waistline	
Waistline Depth from Under Bust	

Strapless bras also have the option of being plunge bras, which generally use a demi wire and a deep separator. These bras will usually have extensive boning for support just as a backless bra would have.

STYLIZED BRA CUP

When creating your own stylized bras, there are two basic methods to changing style lines: measuring and cut & paste. Design concepts can also be adapted to these designs; slash and spread can be used for adding gathering or pintucking.
To assist in creating gathers and pintucks, one can use a variety of specialty feet which will do most of the work for you.

ADJUSTING PATTERNS FOR FIT

When altering patterns for design, many fit issues may arise in the process. There are a few things to look for when checking fit of the cup.

Because woman varies in size and shape, one should check the fit issues mentioned on page 26 prior to adjusting the pattern. The most common issues you will experience when altering the cup shapes will be how the bust fills the cup.

When altering the cup seams, the volume must always remain the same, but certain shapes can affect how a bust fills the shape. Look for these fit issues.

1. If you notice pull lines across the apex and no where else, consider increasing the volume around the center seam or decreasing the volume around the seam ends that are sewn into the band.

2. If you notice pull lines under the apex or above the apex, consider opening up the ends of the seams to increase the volume of the outer cup shape.

3. If you notice extra fabric at the apex, but pulling in other areas, most likely the volume around the edge needs to increase and not decrease the apex area.

CHAPTER 6

NON-WIRED
SOFT BRA

In this chapter, we will convert an underwired bra into a non-wired or soft bra. Both the cup and band pieces are modified to provide more support. For ease in altering the patterns, draw in all of your seam lines 1/4" or .6cm from all edges.

PART 1: PATTERN MANIPULATION

1. Combine the front and back band pieces together overlapping each by their seam allowances of 1/4" or .6cm.

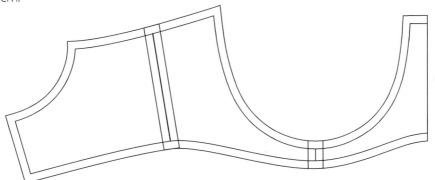

2. Combine the cup pieces together at the side overlapping each by their seam allowances.

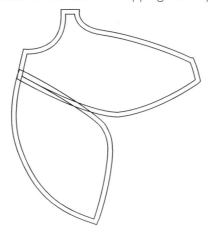

3. Line up the cup sides to the band overlapping each by their seam allowance.

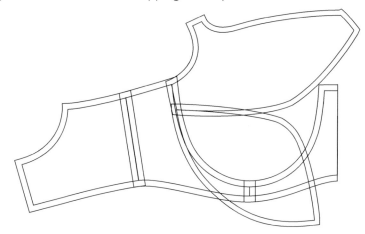

4. Draw a curved shape through the cups to the lower band, leaving the strap point connected to the band.

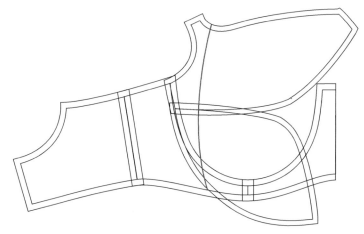

5. Separate the cup on the curved line. Do not disconnect the lower band at this point.

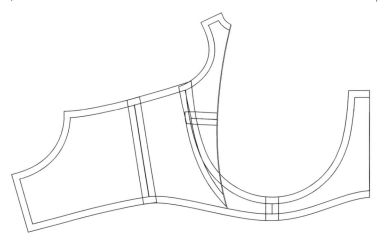

6. Take the lower cup piece that does not line up to the cup curve and cut it apart where the seam lines diverge. Move it inwards to match the seam line on the curve. Make sue not to add space on the actual connecting seam line.

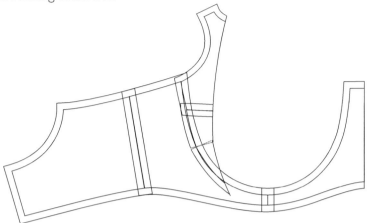

7. Cut the band apart where the cup ends.

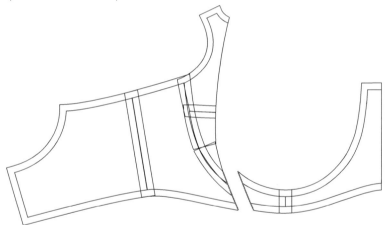

8. Lower the position of the side seam for a straighter waistband. Without underwire, the waistband will provide more support if it is on a straighter plain. Blend all the shapes and add seam allowance to the cup side.

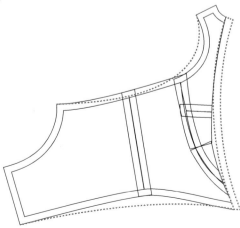

9. a. On the lower front band, draw a straight line from the seam line to the center front neck seam line. Because we are accounting for the seam allowance in the shape, copy the area between the seam allowance and the new seam line. This amount will be added to the cup(s).

    b. Draw a straight line from the lower base at the center of the cup and extend the center front down to meet this point

    c. Add the remaining missing seam allowance at the left side of the lower band.

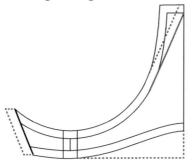

10. Add the section you copied in step 9.a. to the cup(s). Attach to the seam allowance edges. If you attach this to the seam line, you will need to add additional seam allowance. Adding this portion to the edges builds in the missing seam allowance.

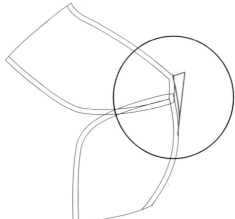

11. Reshape the front neckline to meet the added section. Add the remaining missing seam allowance on the side of the cup pieces.

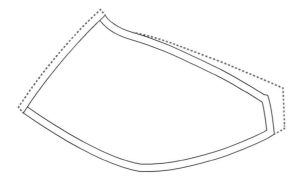
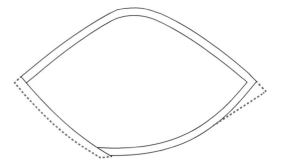

PART 1: CONSTRUCTION

1. Attach cup pieces, finish the center front cup neckline with elastic and the seam with seam tape.

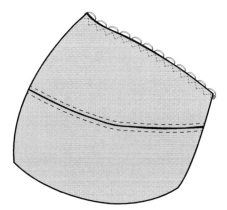

2. Attach the cup to the lower band and cover with seam tape or a thicker underwire channeling for more support.

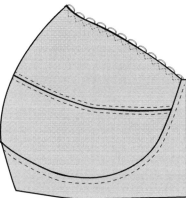

3. Attach elastic to the front neckline section of the band.

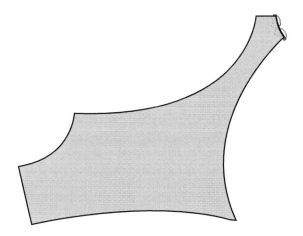

4. Attach the cup/lower band to the back band. Cover the seam with tape or channeling.

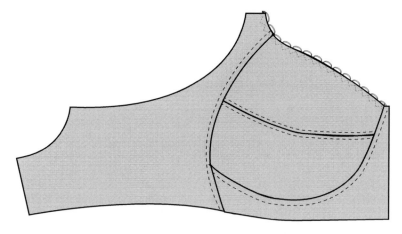

To complete this bra, follow steps 14, 15, 20 and 22-31 from Chapter 2.

CHAPTER 7

NURSING BRA

This chapter examples one design of a nursing bra. These directions make use of the wired design provided with this book.

PART 1: PATTERN MANIPULATION

1. Trace all the cup pattern pieces. You may wish to draw in all the seam lines at 1/4" or .6cm. (This is not pictured.)

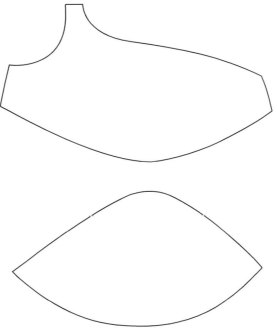

2. The first stage is to create a partial under cup to hold up the breast when the outer cup is unlatched for nursing. At the underarm portion of the cup, temporarily connect the lower cup to the upper cup as pictured, overlapping at the seam allowance.

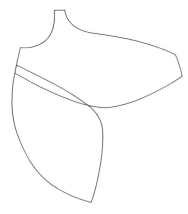

3. From the strap height, measure down 1" or 2.5cm on the neckline towards the center front. On the curve, measure down 2" to 3" or 5cm to 7.5cm (this will vary based on the cup size). Connect the points with a curve and trace off this line and the corresponding neckline shapes. Add a notch to the position where the under cup attaches.

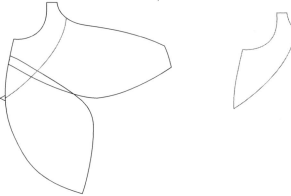

4. Before detaching this cups, shorten the outer cup pieces so there will be some overlap in construction. At the strap height, shorten by 1/2" or 1.25cm. At the cup curve, shorten the cup by 1" or 2.5cm. Draw in this new line.

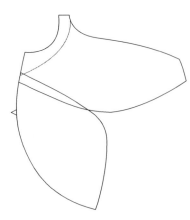

5. Detach the cups at the side and attach the cups at the center front of the cup, overlapping at the seam allowance.

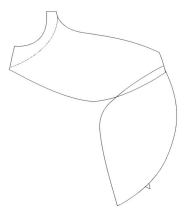

6. Mark 1" or 2.5cm down from the point to 2" to 3" or 5cm to 7.5cm on the center front curve. Trace the new shape.

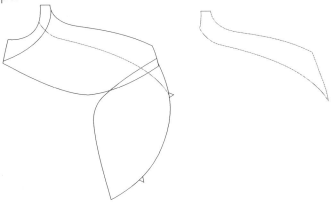

If the joining curve is uneven, smooth out on the new piece.

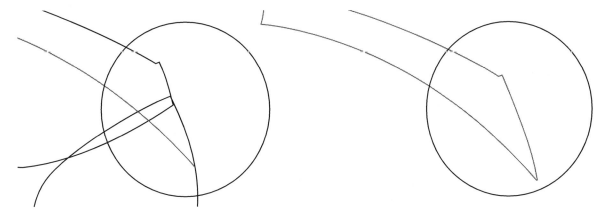

7. Shorten the neckline by taking 1/2" or 1.25cm off at the strap and 1" or 2.5cm off at the center front.

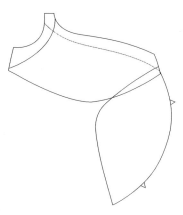

8. Combine the under cup shapes from #3 and #6. At the inner angle, blend out the point with a curve. This will aid in sewing ease.

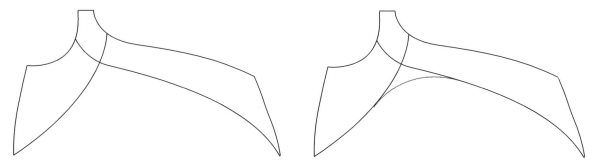

9. On the outer cups, cut off the lines drawn to lower the neckline. In this example, the lower cup did not change, but it does contain two notches.

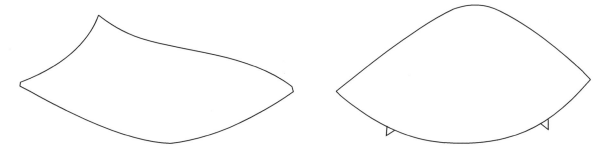

PART 2: CONSTRUCTION METHOD

Complete steps 1-7 from Chapter 2 for the outer cup construction, then complete the following steps.

7. a. On the upper cup, complete the remaining side of the neckline by attaching elastic to the neckline.

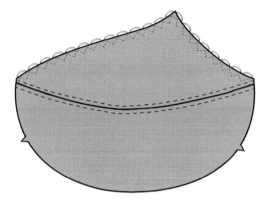

b. On the under cup, attach your elastic to the center front neckline only.

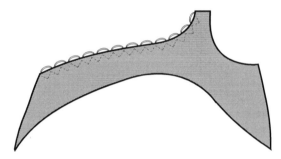

c. On the interior curve on the under cup, either overlock the edge or cover the raw edge with a soft seam tape to avoid irritation. Pictured is an overlock stitch finish.

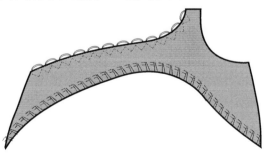

Complete steps 8 through 15 from Chapter 2.

15. a. Place the under cup beneath the upper cup and line up the under cup to the notches. Baste stitch in place at 1/8" or .3cm.

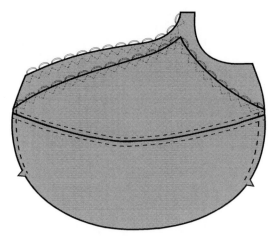

Complete steps 16 through 20 from Chapter 2.

VARIATION 1 - SLIDER HOOK OR NURSING CLIP

20. a. Before attaching the strap to the under cup, take a small loop of fabric and loop it through the slider hook opening or the nursing clip (the slider hook is pictured) and baste stitch in place. Then attach the strap clean finishing the edge of the loop and bar tack in place.

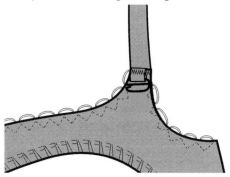

b. Attach a loop of fabric to catch the slider hook on the outer cup and secure with a bar tack. For the second side of the nursing clip, place a smaller loop of fabric through the second portion of the nursing clip.

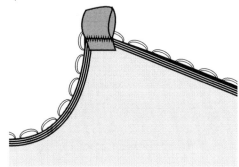

VARIATION 2 - ADJUSTABLE HOOK & EYE

For greater versatility, use a hook and eye tape in place of the slider hook or nursing clip. This will allow for 3 eyes in adjusting the cup as the breast size fluctuates.

20. a. Before attaching the strap to the under cup, place the eye side of the tape to the strap point. Sandwich the tape between the strap and the cup, stitch in place, then fully secure the strap and eye tape with a bar tack.

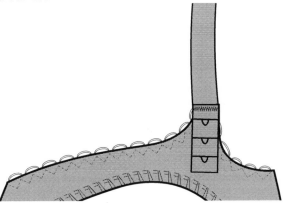

b. Attach the hook side of the tape to the upper cup.

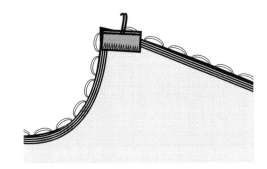

Complete steps 21 through 24 from Chapter 2. For better support, use a hook and eye tape at the center back with an additional column of eyes. With 4 columns of eyes, an individual can adjust for fit up to 2" in width.

CHAPTER 8

MASTECTOMY BRA

Mastectomy bras are regular bras with a pocket for a prosthesis. Depending on whether the customer had a lumpectomy or a full mastectomy, requirements for mastectomy bras will vary. Prosthetics come in a variety of shapes, sizes and coverage. Before designing a bra for mastectomy purposes, determine from the client what shape is required for the pocket. The directions in this chapter demonstrate a full mastectomy pocket.

PART 1: PATTERN MANIPULATION

FITTING INTO A CUP
Determine the size, shape and where the prosthesis sits on the body in proportion to the bra. Some may extend under the arm and some may sit fully in the bra cup. You will need to modify the following directions to accommodate the specific shape.

Your first consideration is to determine if the prosthesis will fit in the bra fully. For a prosthesis that is larger and may tend to need a full coverage cup, you may need to alter the bra cup neckline to accommodate this shape. Pictured here is the altered neckline shape to cover a prosthesis.

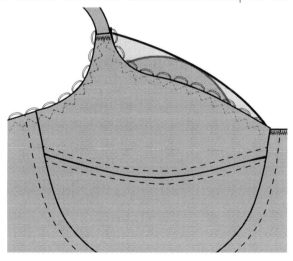

DESIGNING THE POCKET

Determine whether the prosthesis is a complete replacement for the breast or partial. For a complete replacement, you would need to make a flat interior pocket to provide the best support for the prosthesis and the bra. The pocket should be constructed of a soft jersey.

1. Trace the cup and band pieces shown below. I am using the combined band piece for this example. Draw in the 1/4" or .6cm seam allowance as pictured.

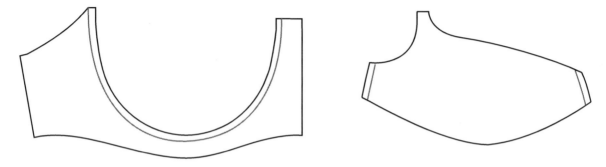

2. Line up the cup top into the band piece at the center front, matching the seam lines.

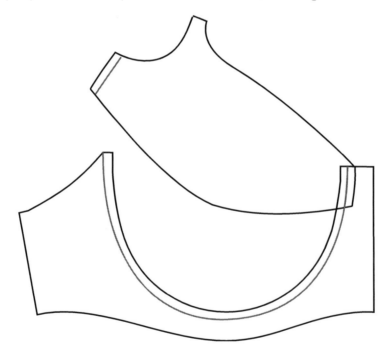

3. Take the left side of the cup and match it to the left side overlapping on the seam lines. This will force the upper cup to take up a dart. Try to keep the exterior lines flat on the table.

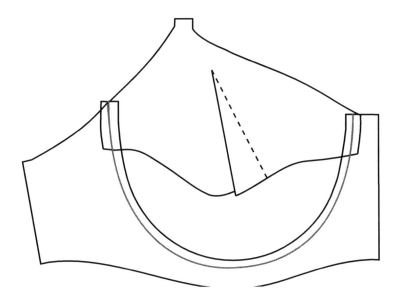

4. Take the new shaped bra piece and copy the neckline, the center half of the underwire curve (plus seam allowance of 1/4" or .6cm) and the side seam. Depending on where the prosthetic sits, you can alter the shape of the pocket.

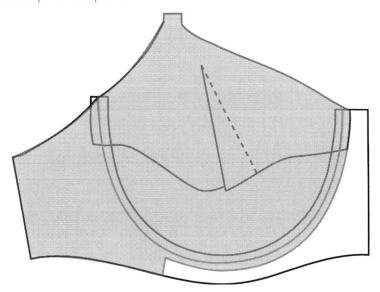

5. Take your pocket piece and remove about 1" or 2.5cm from the armhole. This will be the area where the prosthesis will be inserted.

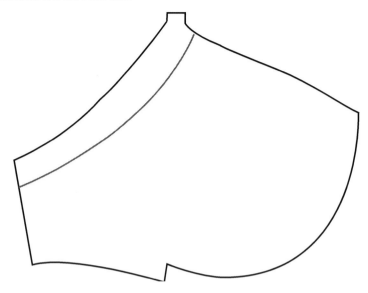

PART 2: CONSTRUCTION DETAILS

The construction steps for including the pocket have a few variations from the basic bra construction. Refer to Chapter 2 for full directions.

1. Finish the pocket opening with an overlock stitch or cover with a seam tape.

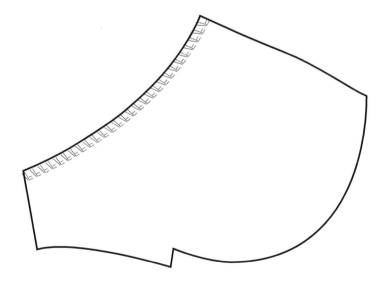

Complete steps 1-5 from Chapter 2, pages 27 and 28.

5. a. Line up the pocket to the neckline and curve of the cup, baste stitch along the edge to secure.

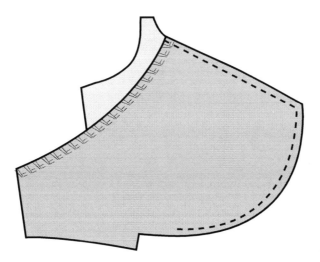

Complete steps 6-13 per the directions from Chapter 2. For attaching a mastectomy pocket, you will need to complete step 16 before steps 12 through 15.

16. a. Attaching the cup will be a little tricky. One will need to attach it in two sections because of the overlapped pocket. After stitching the cup in place, secure the open end of the pocket to the side seam of the front and secure the lower portion to the waistband.

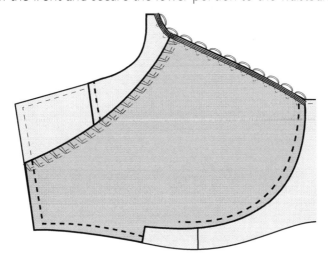

Follow the remaining steps from Chapter 2 to complete this bra.

CHAPTER 9

PADDED BRA

This chapter outlines two types of padding, one being a seamed padded cup and the second is a padded insert which can be added to a cup with a simple pocket.

SEAMED PADDED CUP

This bra contains three distinct pattern sets: the lining, the padding and the design fabric.

PART 1: PATTERN MANIPULATION

1. Trace the cup pieces and draw in the seam allowances or 1/4" or .6cm.

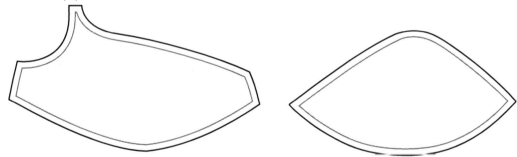

2. Remove the seam allowances and cut these patterns out in a 1/8" or .3cm thick foam or batting.

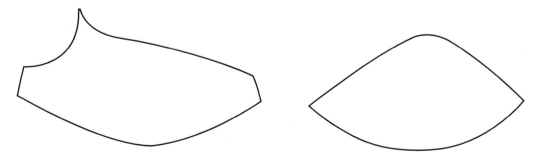

3. For the outer design fabric, take your cup patterns and trace them again. This time, add 1/16" or .15cm around the outer cup edges. This will allow for fitting over the foam batting. If you choose to experiment with different densities and thicknesses of foam or batting, add an amount around the cup equal to 1/2 of the thickness.

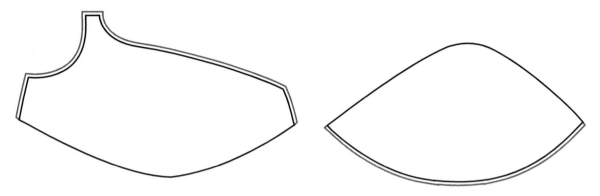

PART 2: CONSTRUCTION

1. Attach each cup (design and lining) together at their center seams as detailed in Chapter 2. Attach the foam cups together with a zigzag stitch. The edges should butt against each other. To attach, slowly ease the two edges together through the machine while stitching the two pieces together.

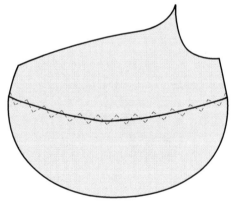

2. Place the elastic of your choice on the design fabric's neckline edge. If using a picot or decorative elastic, attach it with right sides together. If using a clear elastic or plain elastic, attach the elastic to the wrong side at the neckline.

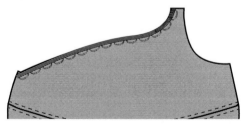

4. With the right side of the lining facing the right side of the design fabric, stitch them together at the neckline.

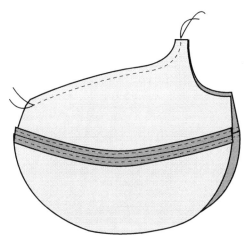

5. Flip them right sides out and under stitch the neckline. An under stitch is when you stitch the seam allowance to the lining side. An under stitch is generally placed right on the edge at 1/16" or 1.5cm away from the seam line.

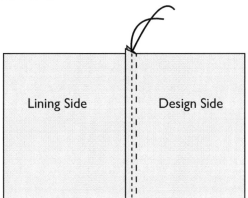

Lining Side   Design Side

6. Place the foam or batting layer between the cup fabric pieces. On the inside of the lining, where the center seam touches the foam, hand tack the center of the seam allowance to the foam. This will keep the lining in place.

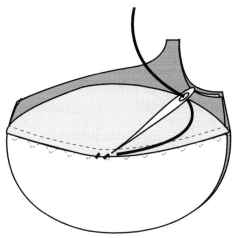

7. Baste stitch the remaining edges together and continue with the bra construction.

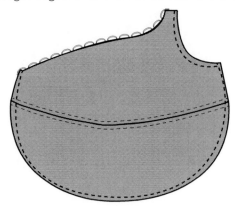

PADDED INSERTS

An alternative to a fully padded cup is to create a padded insert. A pocket similar to a mastectomy pocket can be added into the cup. A soft jersey is recommended for the pocket of the bra.

PART 1: PATTERN MANIPULATION

1. Create the desired shape of the insert. They are generally oval shaped to sit under the bust. This can be used to pad a single side for breast asymmetry or can be used as a push up pad.

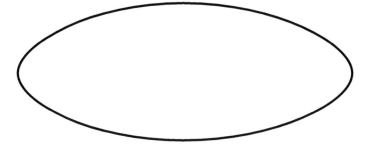

2. Draw in a smaller oval approximately 1/2" or 1.25cm smaller inside the cup. And another one inside that one at about 1/2" or 1.25cm.

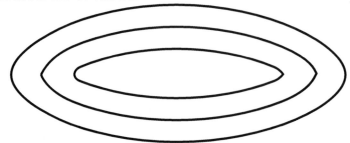

Each of the circles represent a different pattern piece for the batting. For the outer layer, use a thin 1/8" or .3cm batting, for each interior shape you can vary the thicknesses of batting for varied padding.

3. Pockets for padding can be a half lining or a full lining, but the most common is for two pieces to overlap so the insert can be added at leisure. To create this type of pocket, we will create an overlapped seam going vertical on the cup.. Take both the top and bottom cup and trace them off, drawing in their seam allowances.

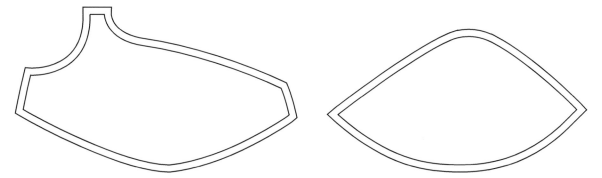

4. Overlap the left sides at the seam allowances. Draw in a curved line away from the apex and then draw a line parallel to the first line 1/2" or 1.25cm to the right. The centers of the cups may overlap a little. We will cut this pattern piece from a jersey with stretch.

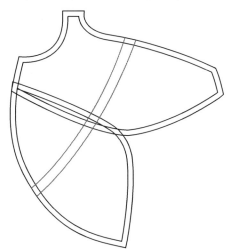

5. Trace the left side with both lines.

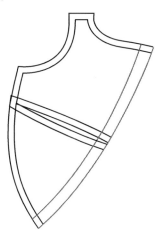

6. Cut off the far left side up to the first line you drew. Separate and line up the right sides at the seam allowance.

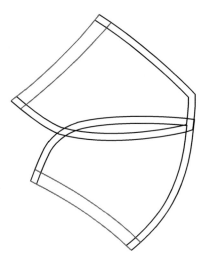

7. Since we aren't technically creating a seamed cup and we are utilizing a jersey for the lining, we don't need to take all the steps detailed later in Chapter 12. The idea behind adding padding to a cup is that the individual wearing the bra doesn't fully fill the cup, so the padded insert will fill the rest of the shaping required of a bra. Create a blended shape for the right side of the cup lining.

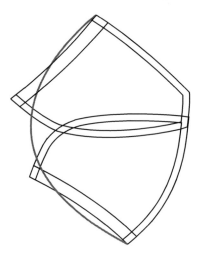

PART 2: CONSTRUCTION

For the padded insert, cut out two layers of the two largest circles and one of the inner layer. Layer the pieces together, top, middle, center, middle, top. To secure each layer, you can use a fabric adhesive or tack the layers together with a hand stitch. When you have completed your construction of the insert, you can stitch around the edges to secure the padded insert in place.

1. To construct the cup lining, cut one left cup and one right cup out of a soft jersey.

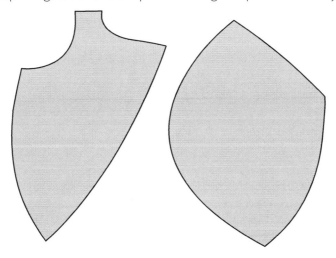

2. Overlap the joining seams at a total of 1/2" or 1.25cm. Baste stitch together to hold in place. The right side of the cup will have excess fabric. This side could be stitched above or below the left side. The insert slides in between the layers.

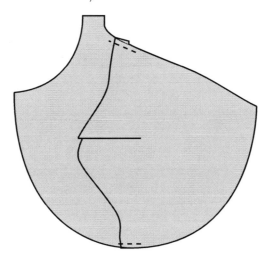

Complete the construction steps in Chapter 3 for completing the construction with lining.

CHAPTER 10

FRONT CLOSURE
DEMI BRA

This chapter alters the neckline of the cup and band for use with a shorter demi wire and front clip closure. There are two directions one can take to approach to alter a pattern for a demi style. This first method starts with the actual demi underwire size. The second method is to design your demi cup and cut a wire to fit.

METHOD 1: UNDERWIRE SIZE

1. Trace the front band and draw in your joining seam allowances at 1/4" or .6cm. Connect the two pieces at the center under cup seam line.

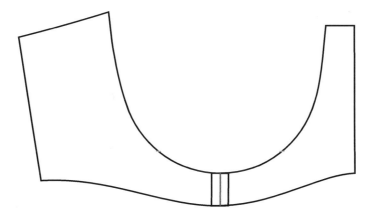

2. Line up the demi underwire under the arm 1/4"to 1/2" (.6cm to 1.25cm) away from the top of the side cup. This allows for elastic attachment and wire movement ease.

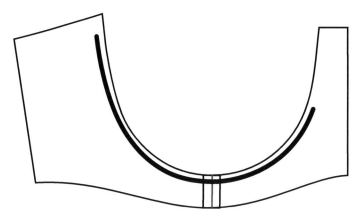

3. Mark on the front neckline where the wire ends. Measure past this point 1/4"to 1/2" (.6cm to 1.25cm) for seam allowance and wire movement.

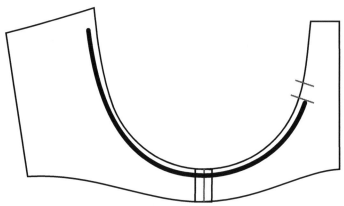

Use the following template and sketch out your new design. Alter your cup design to meet at the center front neckline where the cup ends.

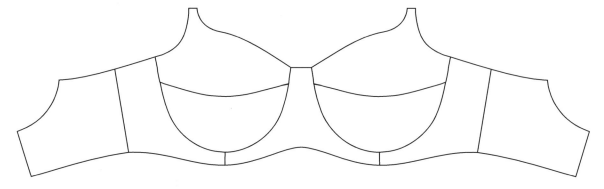

4. The design of this neckline has a descending curve that slopes inwards toward the apex. This neckline shape will show more cleavage and appears as a push up bra, whether or not padding is added.

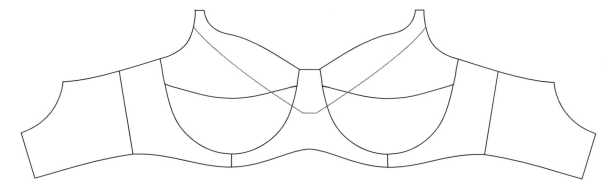

5. a. Determine the size of the clasp for the front. The clasp used in this design is 3/4" or 1.9cm. Add 1/2" or 1.25cm for the seam allowances at the top and bottom (1/4" or .6cm each). The center height for this design totals 1-1/4" or 3.2cm, altering the lower bridge/front band. Note all measurements on your sketch.

    b. The straight edge across the middle measures the width of the clasp which is 3/4" or 1.9cm.

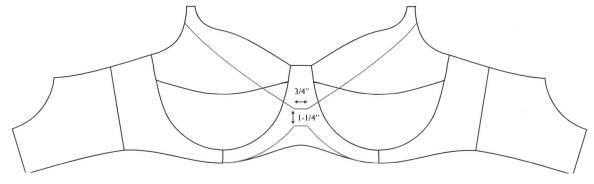

6. Take the cup and band pieces and draw in the seam allowances where they join together.

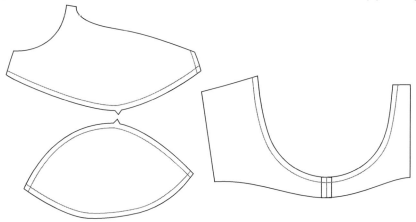

7. Line each of the pattern pieces up at the joining seam lines meeting at the center front. Note that these may not meet perfectly because of the curves on the pattern pieces.

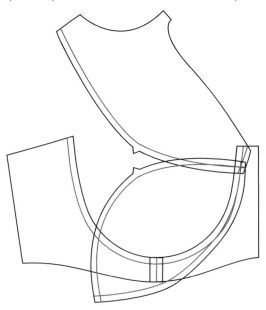

8. Alter your cup and band pattern pieces to meet the specs you decided on. Make sure to match the pattern pieces after separating them and make sure they fit together properly by making sure the joining seam lines all measure the same amount. This is referred to as "walking the seams."

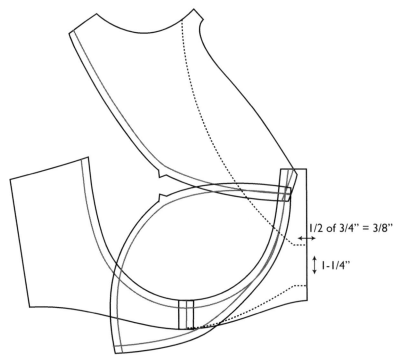

1/2 of 3/4" = 3/8"

1-1/4"

METHOD 2: DESIGN

1. This design differs in that the neckline is sloped upwards for more coverage. This cup's neckline is designed to work as a demi cup on a larger bust size. The clasp for this cup measures 1" or 2.5cm; with seam allowance, the center bridge width is 1-1/2" or 3.8cm.

The width at the center design passes the width of the closure. This amount is not as important as the previous method because it extends past the minimum required size needed for clasp attachment.

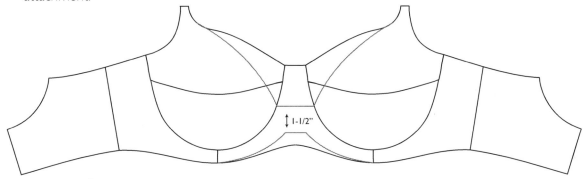

2. Line up the band and cup pieces at their seam lines and alter the pattern to the specifications of the design.

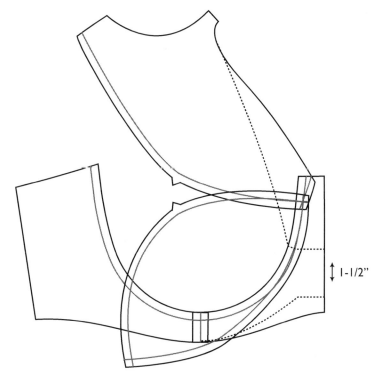

3. Line up your full underwire to the band leaving 1/4" to 1/2" (.6cm to 1.25cm) spacing at the underarm. Mark on the underwire where the neckline of the band ends. Shorten the underwire by an additional 1/4"to 1/2" (.6cm to 1.25cm) at the center neckline.

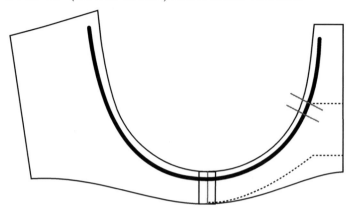

To keep the underwire from poking through the garment, use an epoxy dip, Household Goop, or a similar product on the cut end.

CHAPTER II

STRAPLESS BRA

This chapter examples two variations of a strapless bra. The first creates a basic strapless design, while the second creates a backless style. Both styles may need additional support in the cups. If this is the case, it is recommended you create a padded cup following the steps from Chapter 9.

PART I: PATTERN MANIPULATION

VARIATION I: BASIC STRAPLESS

I. Trace the top cup of the basic bra.

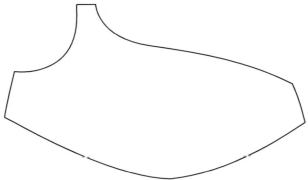

2. Curve the top of the cup as pictured or to the style of your design.

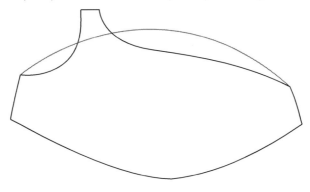

Optional: After sewing your first sample, some fitting may need to be done to make sure the breast tissue is held firmly into the cup. You may potentially need to alter the cup shape to better house the bust. This can be done by taking in darts towards the seam line. Once darts are closed securely tape them closed and reshape the neckline.

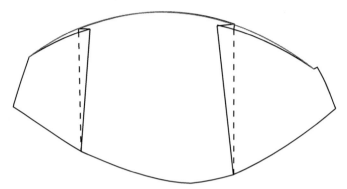

4. Trace all the basic bra band pattern pieces. The bra band pictured here was modified from the design provided in the book. These directions can be modified for most band shapes. Draw in the 1/4" or .6cm seam allowance at the side seams and front band.

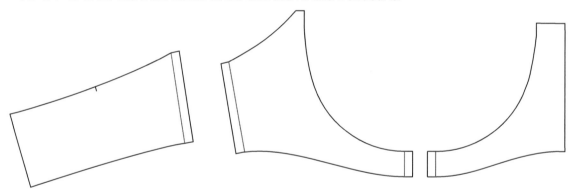

5. Combine each of the seams, overlapping them at the seam allowances.

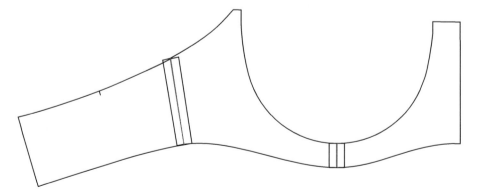

6. A strapless bra hugs the body without the use of a strap. It generally sits higher under the arm then a basic bra. Extend the center front of the band down to the lowest point of the front band. Square a line across all the way to the center back and square a line up so it touches the furthest extended center back seam.

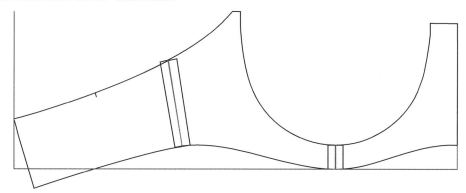

7. Square a line across from the side of the cup to the center back.

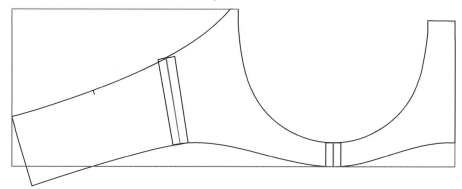

8. Draw in a new side seam from where the top of the side seam hits. This position will vary based on the original band design this draft is using. Actual side seams can be adjusted during a test fit.

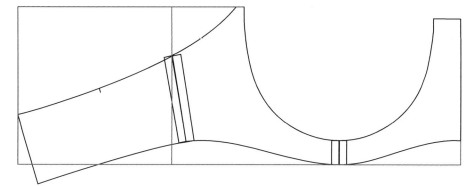

9. Determine the number of hooks & eyes desired for the bra. This chart includes seam allowance for the top and bottom.

Rows	Centimeters	Inches
1	3.2	1.25
2	4.5	1.75
3	5.8	2.25
4	7.1	2.75
5	8.4	3.25
6	9.7	3.75

10. Find the middle on the center back line. This will mark the center of the back closure. Mark the width of the hook & eye tape on the back line.

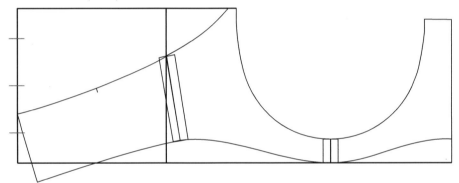

11. a. Draw in a gentle curve from the top of the side cup to the hook & eye top.

b. Draw in a gradual curve from the bottom of the cup band to the bottom of the hook & eye tape. During fitting, if the band cuts too far into the underarm, lower the center back slightly so the underarm curve also lowers.

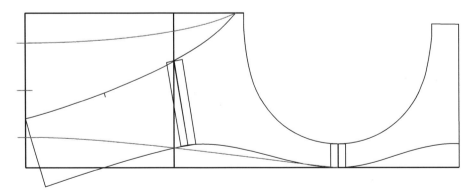

For construction steps, refer to Chapter 2. Complete steps 1-5, skip 6 and 7, continue with steps 8-21 and 30-31. Using a gripper elastic is recommended for attaching the elastic to the neckline. Adding padding to the cup is also recommended. Combine the steps in Chapter 9 with those in Chapter 2 to complete this bra.

VARIATION 2 - BACKLESS STRAPLESS

Follow steps 1-3 on page 97 and 98 and continue with the following steps to develop the backless variation. For this style, a longer band or base is required.

4. Trace the band bra patterns, draw in the seam allowances and connect at the seam lines. Sketch in the seam allowance at the center back.

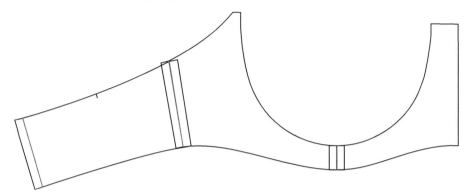

5. Take the measurements recorded from page 62.

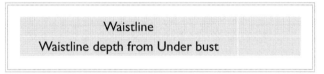

Waistline	
Waistline depth from Under bust	

6. Square a line across from the bottom of the center of the cup to the center front.

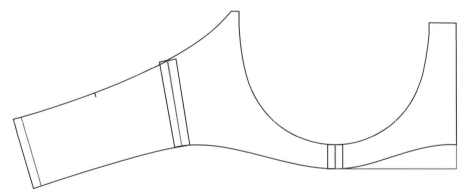

7. From the line at center front, measure down the waistline depth. At the depth, square a line across 1/4 of the waistline measurement. This will mark the bottom of the side seam. Draw a line from the top of the side seam to the side of the waistline.

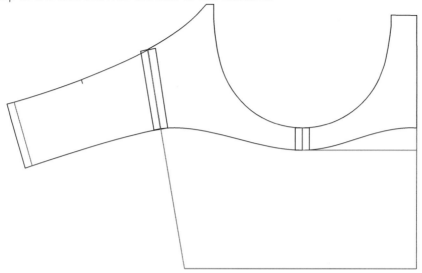

8. The back of a bra is designed for stretch. The back of the bras also contains a hook & eye closure. Because of these items, the 1/4 waistline measurement must be altered to accommodate these items. Subtract 7/8" or 1.9cm for the hook & eye, then multiply by .75 for the reduction of stretch. In the Advanced section, fabrics with stretches different from those described in the Beginner section will be discussed in further detail.

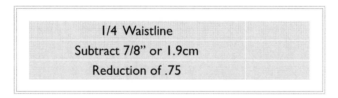

1/4 Waistline	
Subtract 7/8" or 1.9cm	
Reduction of .75	

9. Square a line across from the side seam towards the back the reduced measurement from step 8.

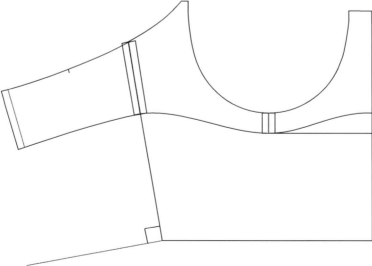

10. From the top of the center back pattern, draw a line down to the back of the waistline.

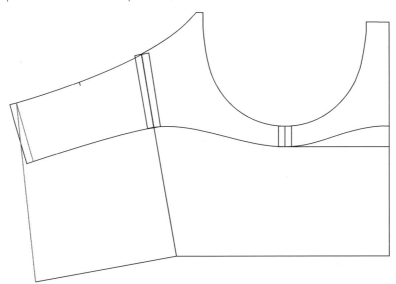

11. Drop the center back the length of distance you wish for a backless style, keeping in mind the sizes needed for hook & eye tape (refer to the table on page 100). For this example, I left 3-1/4" or 8.4cm for a five row hook & eye closure. Curve the waistline to remove the sharp angles and for better body contouring.

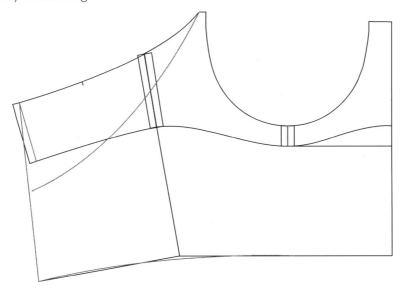

12. Add seam allowance to the center back and at the side seam. Add a notch at the center of the cup.

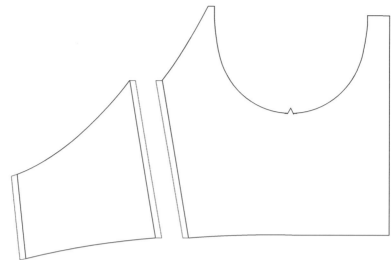

13. The last step is to determine where boning needs to be placed other than the side seam. This can vary depending on how low you dip the back. All boning must be placed in a straight line since it is rigid and is not flexible from side to side.

    a. In this example, 4 boning pieces will be added to the front and 2 on the back, plus an additional piece of boning at the side seam. Boning pieces can be angled or in a straight line. The angled layout will provide for more comfort when seated. This quantity of boning is not always necessary, as it will depend on the support needed for the wearer. Smaller cup sizes will not need the same amount of structure that a large cup needs.

    b. To mark where the boning placement goes, place notches at the beginning and end of each boning piece. These notches can be inward or outward depending on your precision in cutting/sewing. Drill holes can also be used to indicate boning placement. Drill holes are generally circled in red and are placed 1/8" to 1/4" (.3cm to .6cm) away from the placement.

    c. Indicate the length of boning and casing needed for each on the pattern. Remove the 1/4" or .6cm seam allowance off both ends for precise cuts.

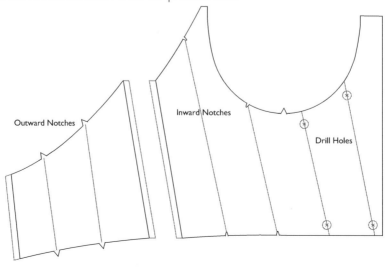

PART 2: CONSTRUCTION

Follow the steps recommended for the basic strapless bra with the following inclusion.

13. d. After attaching the boning to the side seam, stitch both sides of the casing for each boning placement to the band leaving a 1/4" or .6cm gap at the top and bottom for seam allowance. Use wither the notches as a guide or the drill holes. For a drill hole, line up the top and bottom of the casing, then stitch in place.

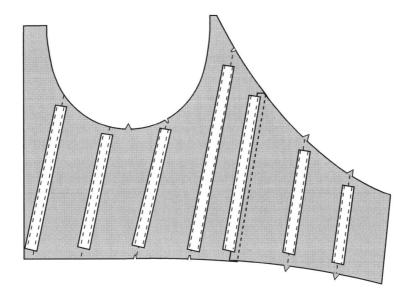

CHAPTER 12

STYLIZING A BRA: SEAM LINES

There are endless possibilities for the style lines one can create. This chapter explores two different methods to achieve seam line changes using the three piece cup from Chapter 3. These directions can also be modified for use with the two piece cup.

CHANGING STYLE LINES

METHOD 1: MEASURING

1. Trace the three piece cup. Next to your traced off pieces, sketch the stylized cup you wish to create. For example purposes, we will modify the design to the one pictured.

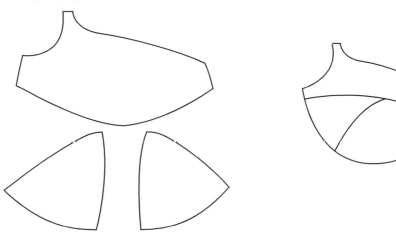

2. List all of your cup modifications. As per this example, these are the changes.

   a. The left side of the upper cup is narrower.

   b. The apex height is raised. In this example, it is raised 1/2" or 1.25cm. This type of change will create a bullet bra appearance leaving a slightly pointy apex.

   c. The lower right cup size has increased in width, making the lower left cup smaller.

3. Mark your estimated changes on the upper cup. Note that even though the style line is curved upwards in the sketch, the curve is in a downward slope on the pattern. These types of changes will need to be sewn and fit to determine if he style line sits where desired.

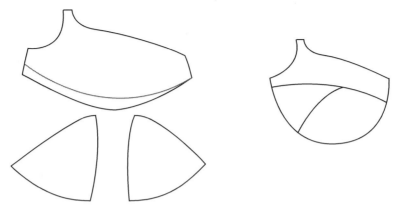

4. Measure the amounts of change on the upper cup and make the corresponding changes to the lower cup. This means where you take away 1/2" or 1.25cm from one cup piece, add it to the other cup piece. Make sure to measure the new lines and make sure they match equally.

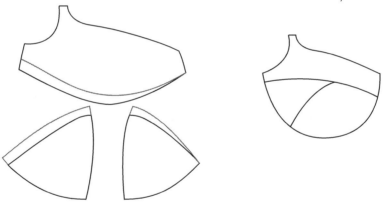

5. The next change is to modify the style lines of the lower cups. Draw in your lower left cup change.

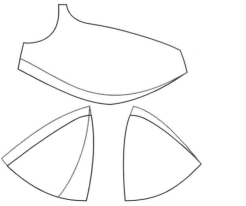

6. Measure and move the style line of the lower right cup. Make sure to measure and walk the new seam lines to make sure they match in length. If you are using the patterns provided with this book, seam allowance is included. The seam lines are actually 1/4" or .6cm from the edges of the pattern pieces.

METHOD 2: CUT AND PASTE

1. a. Trace the three piece cup and sketch your new design to the right. This design contains a side bust stabilizer, which gives greater support to the larger cup.

   b. Draw in your inner seam allowances of 1/4" or .6cm.

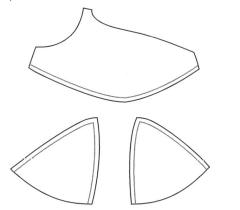
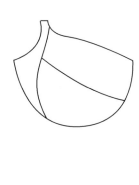

2. On top of the sketch, draw in your original seam lines as a reference.

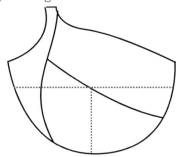

3. Starting with the top cup, draw where the seam is split and cut the top cup apart.

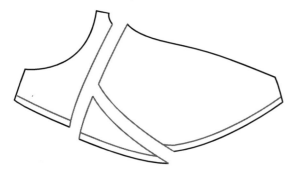
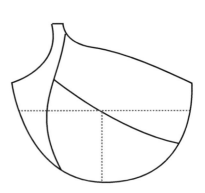

4. Take the far left piece of the top cup and tape it to the lower cup lining it up the seam lines. Where the top piece is added, extend the new seam line through the lower left cup and separate. Smooth out all the points with a smooth curve. On your sketch, check off each joined seam to keep track of the changes.

Adjusted Pattern

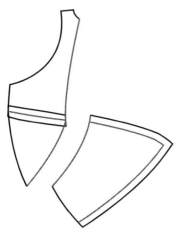

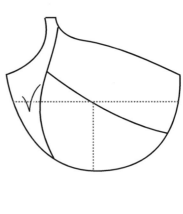

5. Combine the upper center piece to the lower center piece by overlapping at the seam line. Notice at the right side, the curved seam lines do not meet. To fix this, take the average of the points to achieve the correct shape as pictured in the adjusted pattern.

Adjusted Pattern

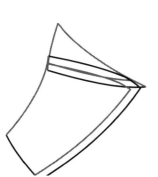
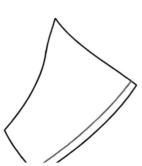
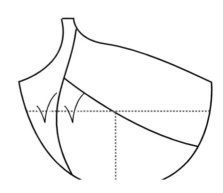

6. Combine the middle piece we created in step 5 to the lower right pattern piece at the seam line. Note that the top of the center piece doesn't have seam allowance, but the lower right side does. Use the seam line for adjusting the shape, not the seam allowance line. You may wish to cut off the seam allowance on this portion of the pattern.

The gap at the apex of both of these pieces is expansive. By taking the average space in between, we would be lengthening the two upper joining seams. This is not desired because the patterns will no longer fit together. By taking in the average apex point, we will need to also utilize the first concept of measuring. The amount we take in at the center, remove off both sides and blend in a new shape. The most important thing to remember is that the seam lines need to remain consistent and match the adjoining pattern pieces.

Adjusted Pattern

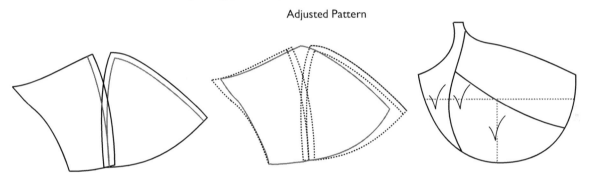

7. There is one more step that needs to be done on the lower right piece. Looking at the style lines on the design, draw in the seam line for the pattern change.

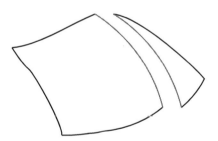
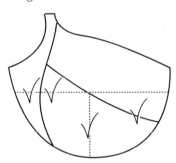

8. Combine the remaining top right piece to the lower right piece. We removed the seam allowance off the joining seam in step 6, so be careful to line up the seam lines of the both pieces. The top piece still has seam allowance. You can adjust the seam lines as we did in step 6 or you can modify one side as shown below. Each change and modification will alter the way the bra fits, so test and fit different methods to see which achieves the best fit for your customer. There is no "one right way" to achieve results.

Note: The volume of the cup remains the same whether we use the method in step 6 or 8, the difference will be where the style lines sit on the body.

Adjusted Pattern

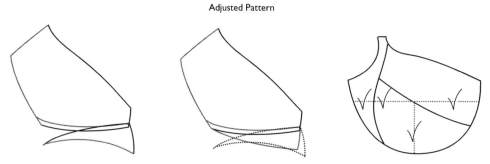

9. Note the shapes and evaluate the order you will construct the cup. For this design, I have numbered the seams in the order I would construct this cup. Because of the shapes of seam #1, this cup will initially create a pointed shape. Blend out all awkward points by taking averages with your curve as pictured. This design may need multiple fit samples to achieve a proper fit.

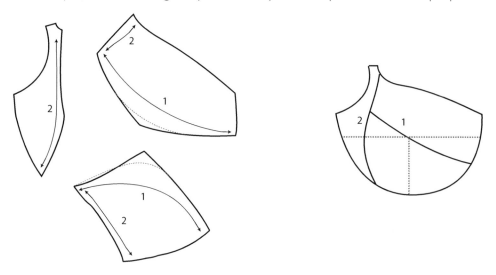

The last step will be to add the joining seam allowances of 1/4" or .6cm back into the pattern pieces.

CHAPTER 13

STYLIZING A BRA: SLASH AND SPREAD

Gathering and pintucking details can be added to any cup. The following steps are simple changes that utilize the concept of slash and spread.

GATHERS

Decide on the amount of gathers preferred. These steps utilize a two to one gathering ratio, meaning there will be twice as much fabric that will be gathered into the actual shape.

PART 1: PATTERN MANIPULATION

1. Take the pattern piece and draw a variety of evenly spaced lines across the piece in the direction you want to span the gathers.

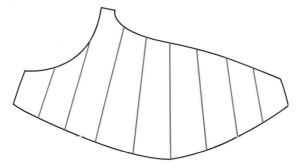

2. Cut the pieces apart and space them equally apart keeping each divided line parallel to the next. Space them so the total amount of the new pattern is twice the original pattern.

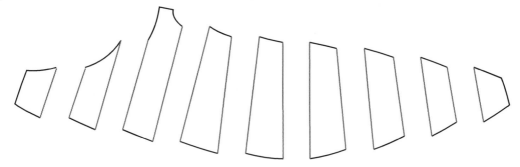

3. Draw in the new seam lines, averaging each point.

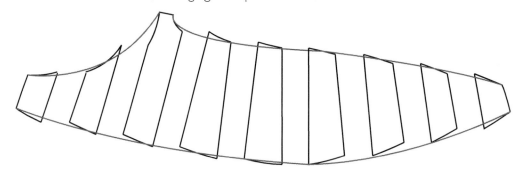

PART 2: CONSTRUCTION

1. Cut out the original pattern piece and the gathered pattern piece. The original piece can be cut out of a tricot lining fabric to reduce bulk. The two layers will be treated as one when constructing the cup.

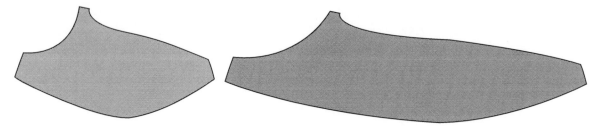

2. Run a basting stitch on the larger pattern piece at 1/8" or .3cm on each section to be gathered. This can be done by machine or by hand.

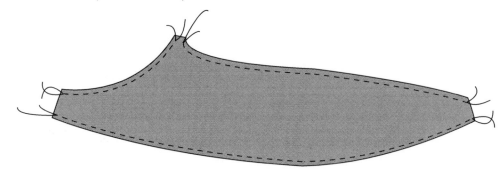

3. Pull the gathering stitches and match the gathered piece to the lining piece. Once you have them pulled equally, baste stitch the gathered cup to the flat cup at 1/8" or .3cm and continue constructing the cup as directed in the Beginner section.

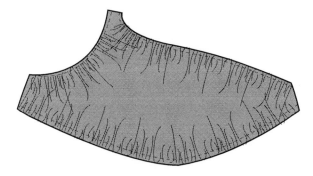

PINTUCKS

Determine the size and spacing of your pintucks. For this example, I will place 1/8" or .3cm pintucks 1" or 2.5cm apart.

PART 1: PATTERN MANIPULATION

1. Take the pattern piece and draw straight lines parallel to each other 1" or 2.5cm apart across the pattern piece.

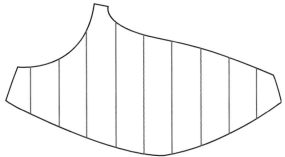

2. Because the pintucks are 1/8" or .3cm when stitched, they are 1/4" or .6cm before stitching. Cut each piece apart and space them 1/4" or .6cm apart, parallel to each other.

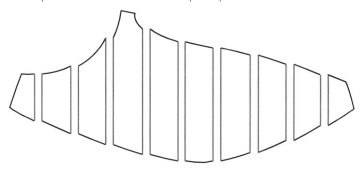

3. Determine which direction the pintucks will lay when fully constructed For this example, we will fold the pintucks away from the center front. This information is needed to create the shape of the space in between each pintuck. This is called the uptake shape.

To create the uptake shape, fold the two edges of the pintuck together then fold towards the side seam. Use your pinpoint tracing wheel to roll over the original shape of the pattern. The dotted markings on the paper, once you open it back up, is the uptake shape.

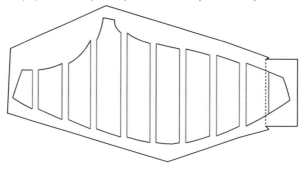

PART 2: CONSTRUCTION

1. Fold the fabric at the beginning and end of each pintuck and stitch at the pintuck size. This example is stitched at 1/8" or .3cm.

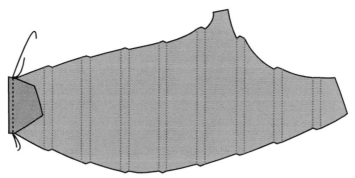

2. After completing all the pintucks, press them to the side indicated by the pattern and stitch down in place around the edges. Construct the remainder of the cup as shown in the Beginner section.

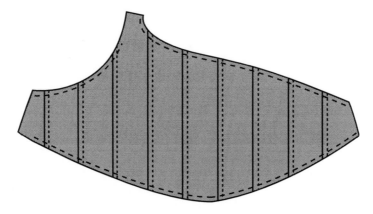

ADVANCED

CHAPTER 14

INTRODUCTION TO PATTERN DRAFTING AND GRADING

The Beginner and Intermediate sections of this book have introduced several construction and pattern manipulation concepts.

The Advanced section guides one through drafting a basic bra, creating patterns from your drafts and grading your patterns into sizes.

TOOLS

Compass - A compass is a two pronged mathematical device that creates a perfect circle. It will be necessary in drafting both the cup and the band.

Calculator - Having a basic calculator handy is a must when dealing with the intricacies of the bra and it's components.

Flexible Ruler - This is a flexible/bendable ruler that you can use to measure curves. This is recommended when measuring the cup for accuracy.

Oaktag, Manila or Hard tag paper - Depending on where one is in the world, this may have different names. This paper is thick like poster board and generally manila in color. It is used to finalize patterns and is used for creating slopers. Alternately, you can use poster board if you do not have access to actual tag paper.

TERMINOLOGY

Production Patterns - Production patterns are replications of your final patterns made in tag paper. We use these to trace off the outlines onto a large sheet of paper called a marker. If you are making these for home use only, I would recommend making a hard paper pattern as a backup to your paper patterns.

Markers - Markers are paper layouts of all your pattern pieces. It is used to conserve fabric in cutting, to keep the pattern pieces on the correct grain of the fabric and to produce an accurate estimate of how much fabric is used in the garment.

Slopers - A sloper (or block pattern) is a basic pattern shape used in creating designs. It does not have seam allowance and is created for the sample size. This is a drafting term and is not something you may be familiar with if you are not in the fashion industry.

FABRICS AND STRETCH

In the Beginner section, we discussed the stretch of the fabrics recommended for the patterns included with this book.

Your specific fabric selections may vary from those mentioned previously. In this section you will develop your own patterns based on the stretch of your chosen fabrics.

Test the fabric for stretch in the same manner as stated in the Beginner section. A printed tape measure is provided in this book on page 18.

Fabric should not be reduced by its full amount of stretch, but only by a percentage of its stretch. The following chart will be used by multiplying the body's measurements by the stretch multiplier. Further directions are included in the chapters following.

Based on how much the fabric stretches from 5" or 10cm, you can use the stretch reduction chart on the following page. It is recommended you reduce your measurement by 50% for the bra back band, but 40% and 45% are provided for your convenience. The following chapter refers to this chart.

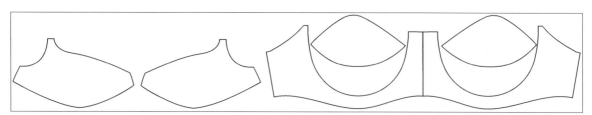

Marker for Bra Front Fabric

STRETCH REDUCTION CHART FOR FABRIC

Amount Stretched	Stretch Ratio	40% Multiplier	45% Multiplier	50% Multiplier
5 1/4	5%	0.9800	0.9775	0.9750
5 1/2	10%	0.9600	0.9550	0.9500
5 3/4	15%	0.9400	0.9325	0.9250
6	20%	0.9200	0.9100	0.9000
6 1/4	25%	0.9000	0.8875	0.8750
6 1/2	30%	0.8800	0.8650	0.8500
6 3/4	35%	0.8600	0.8425	0.8250
7	40%	0.8400	0.8200	0.8000
7 1/4	45%	0.8200	0.7975	0.7750
7 1/2	50%	0.8000	0.7750	0.7500
7 3/4	55%	0.7800	0.7525	0.7250
8	60%	0.7600	0.7300	0.7000
8 1/4	65%	0.7400	0.7075	0.6750
8 1/2	70%	0.7200	0.6850	0.6500
8 3/4	75%	0.7000	0.6625	0.6250
9	80%	0.6800	0.6400	0.6000
9 1/4	85%	0.6600	0.6175	0.5750
9 1/2	90%	0.6400	0.5950	0.5500
9 3/4	95%	0.6200	0.5725	0.5250
10	100%	0.6000	0.5500	0.5000
10 1/4	105%	0.5800	0.5275	0.4750
10 1/2	110%	0.5600	0.5050	0.4500
10 3/4	115%	0.5400	0.4825	0.4250
11	120%	0.5200	0.4600	0.4000
11 1/4	125%	0.5000	0.4375	0.3750
11 1/2	130%	0.4800	0.4150	0.3500
11 3/4	135%	0.4600	0.3925	0.3250
12	140%	0.4400	0.3700	0.3000
12 1/4	145%	0.4200	0.3475	0.2750
12 1/2	150%	0.4000	0.3250	0.2500
12 3/4	155%	0.3800	0.3025	0.2250
13	160%	0.3600	0.2800	0.2000

WIRE SIZING

The following chart was compiled by taking average measurements from several different wire manufacturers. These wire sizes are the exact size that are available from our publisher at www.losangelesfashionresource.com.

In the following chapter, use this wire chart to determine the diameter of the wire. These measurements increase by 5/16" or .8cm.

Wire Size	Wire Diameter (Imperial)	Wire Diameter (Metric)
28	3 9/16	9.0
30	3 7/8	9.8
32	4 3/16	10.6
34	4 1/2	11.4
36	4 13/16	12.2
38	5 1/8	13.0
40	5 7/16	13.7
42	5 3/4	14.5
44	6	15.3
46	6 5/16	16.1
48	6 5/8	16.9
50	6 15/16	17.7
52	7 1/4	18.5
54	7 9/16	19.3
56	7 7/8	20.0
58	8 3/16	20.8
60	8 1/2	21.6

PATTERNS AND LABELING

Patterns are generally labeled with a variety of information including Style Name, Piece Name, Size and Cut Number. For tracking, I advise the use of a stamp with all contact information included on it. Stamp each pattern piece. This is important when contracting work out. You don't want your patterns to end up in someone else's hands.

Patterns should be marked with grainlines to indicate the length grain of the pattern for proper orientation when marker making and cutting.

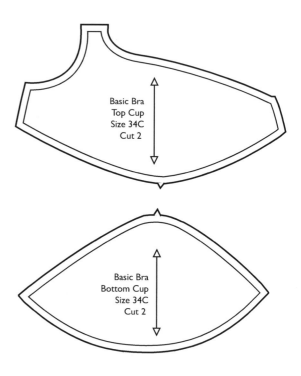

Basic Bra
Top Cup
Size 34C
Cut 2

Basic Bra
Bottom Cup
Size 34C
Cut 2

GRADING AND GRADE RULES

Grading is a term that is used in reference to creating a size range. Grading is a very complicated subject and varies depending on the garment. This book explores the grading methods for a basic bra.

When beginning your venture in grading, you will first need to define your size chart. I recommend you use the information in this book, including the size charts and adapt a size chart appropriate for your country and your base customer.

When developing a measurement chart for sizes, one is actually creating a basic grade rules chart

BASIC GRADING FOR WOVEN GARMENTS

Cup sizes increase and decrease in size by 1/2" in the US, 1.25cm in the UK, Europe and other international countries, and 1cm in Australia.

Bands sizes increase and decrease by 2" in the US and 5cm everywhere else.

	Cup Volume	Band Width
US	1/2"	2"
UK/Euro	1.25cm	5cm
Australia	1cm	5cm

BASIC GRADING FOR STRETCH GARMENTS

After creating the basic woven grade rule, a stretch grade must be developed for the bra back.

For the patterns included in this book, I based my stretch measurements on power netting which contains a 50% stretch. You are under no obligation to use a power net, but you should use a fabric with great stretch and stability. It is not recommended to use a stretch fabric for the front of a bra.

The following stretch grade chart is based on a power net stretch.

	1/4 Band	1/2 Band
US	3/8"	3/4"
UK/Euro	.94cm	1.88cm
Australia	.94cm	1.88cm

Use the following chart to create a custom grade rule for a specific fabric.

CUSTOM CHART		
Fabric	1/4 Band	1/2 Band

CHAPTER 15

BRA BAND
PATTERN DRAFTING

The directions for the bra band are broken into 3 parts: cup, front band and back band. The following chapter will cover the drafting of the cup based on the results of the band draft.

CUP DRAFT

For ease in drafting directions, the draft is of the left side of the garment with the center front seam on the right side. If you choose to draft both the left and right side, reverse the direction of the draft for the right side of the garment. Many individuals have two different size breasts. To make a custom bra, draft both the right and left sides of the bra.

1. Using the charts on pages 24 and 25, choose the most appropriate wire sizes. Refer to the wire diameter chart on page 122.

Left Bust Diameter		Right Bust Diameter	
Left Bust Wire Size		Right Bust Wire Size	
Wire Diameter		Wire Diameter	

2. Draw a square using the diameter of the underwire as the height and width. Label the right vertical line Center Front.

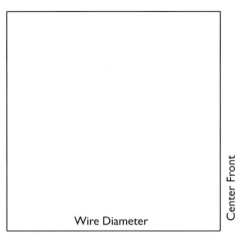

3. Divide the wire diameter in half both vertically and horizontally.

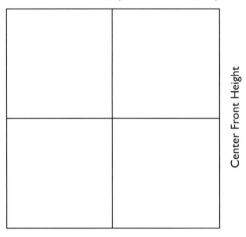

4. Take your compass and line up the point at the center mark and the pencil up to the center bottom line. Make a full circle with your compass. If you marked everything correctly, the edges of the circle should touch the top, right, left and bottom lines exactly.

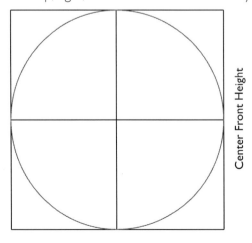

5. On the right side, draw a line parallel to the first line you drew 3/4" or 1.9cm to the right. Extend the top, middle and bottom lines to reach this new line. This is for spacing between the breasts. This amount is pretty standard, but for design variations, one can experiment by using a smaller amount.

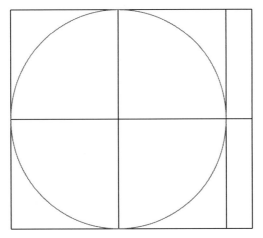

6. On the original center front line on the right, measure up 1/2" or 1.25cm and square a line across towards the new right line 1/8" or .3cm.

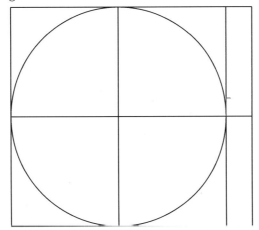

7. Blend the bottom part of the circle to meet the 1/8" or .3cm mark with a slightly curved line.

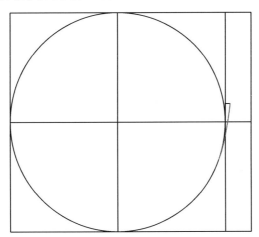

8. On the left side of the center line, measure up 3/4" or 1.9cm and square out to the left 1/4" or .6cm.

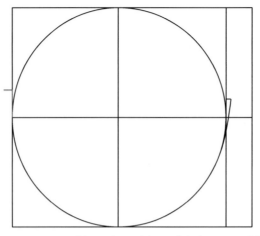

9. Blend the bottom of the curve up to this point with a slightly curved line.

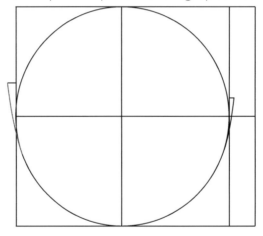

Because steps 6-9 could vary depending on the wire you purchase, once you have this base compare your wire to the curve you created. If your wires are longer, I would consider cutting the wire down to the height shown here.

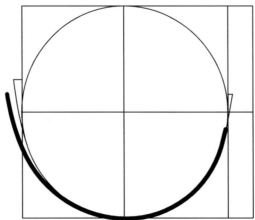

For shorter wires, adjust the curve by marking the new height rise. For wires that extend further out to the left, redraw the end of your curve. Manufacturers of wires are not always consistent when it comes to height and width of wires.

These drafting directions took the average amounts and made them consistent in growth and size.

FRONT BAND

10. Take the chest and under bust measurements from page 21 and divide each by 4 to indicate 1/4 of the body.

Chest Measurement	1/4 Chest Measurement
Under Bust Measurement	1/4 Under Bust Measurement

11. Take the wire diameter measurement and subtract it from 1/4 of the chest and under bust measurements.

Left	**Right**
1/4 Chest	1/4 Chest
Subtract Left Wire Diameter	Subtract Right Wire Diameter
New Chest Measurement	New Chest Measurement
1/4 Under Bust	1/4 Under Bust
Subtract Left Wire Diameter	Subtract Right Wire Diameter
New Under Bust Measurement	New Under Bust Measurement

STRETCH VARIATION

11. If you wish to use a stretch fabric for the front band, take your new measurements and multiply by the stretch multiplier on page 121 to get your new amount. This will be the same number you will use for the back.

Stretch Multiplier	
New Chest Measurement	Reduced Chest Measurement
New Under Bust Measurement	Reduced Under Bust Measurement

12. On the left line, measure from the top out, the balance of the chest measurement from step 11, at the bottom line measure out the balance of the under bust measurement.

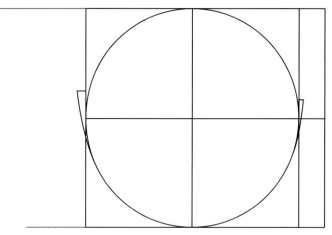

13. Connect the two lines together at the ends.

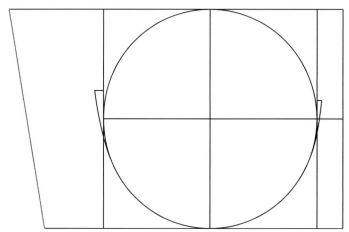

BACK BAND

14. a. For the back of the band, we will begin in the same manner as the front, taking 1/4 of both the chest and under bust measurements.

Chest Measurement		1/4 of Chest Measurement	
Under Bust Measurement		1/4 of Under Bust Measurement	

b. Because the back also contains a hook & eye and the hook & eye is not part of the back band pattern piece, remove the amount needed for a hook & eye. On average, the amount is 1-3/4" or 4.5cm (at the hook's tightest, it is 1" or 2.5cm and at its loosest, it is 2-1/2" or 6.4cm). Because this draft is for half the body, divide the average amount by two, so 1-3/4 would be 7/8" (4.5cm would be 2.25cm).

> **Back Chest Bust – Hook & Eye**
> **Back Under Bust – Hook & Eye**

c. Because a snug fit is needed, take the stretch of the fabric into account. Using the stretch ratio charts found on page 121, reduce your back measurements based on the stretch of the fabric (.75 for power netting).

> **Reduced Back Chest**
> **Reduced Back Under Bust**

15. Continue the back band draft on the front draft. At the new slanted line we created in step 14, square a line across at 90 degrees, the reduced chest measurement and the under bust measurement in their respective positions.

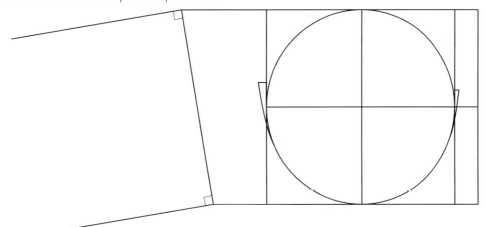

16. Connect the ends of the two lines together with a straight line. This is the center back line.

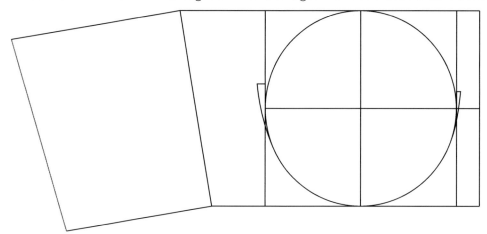

17. At the center back, from the bottom of the line measure up the distance from the chart below based on how many rows of hooks & eyes you require.

Rows	Centimeters	Inches
1	1.9	0.75
2	3.2	1.25
3	4.5	1.75
4	5.8	2.25
5	7.1	2.75
6	8.4	3.25

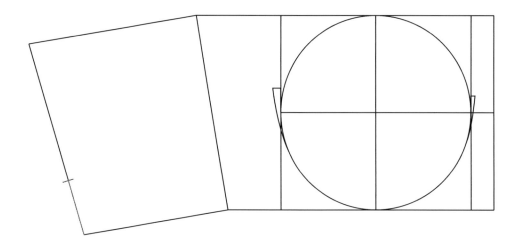

18. Where the front meets the back or the side seam, measure up an amount between 1/8" and 3/4" or .3cm and 1.9cm. This is to help in the shaping of the bra. This amount can be modified to fit your design specifications. For a strapless bra, you may wish to keep this measurement on the smaller side. As pictured, the side was raised by 1/4" or .6cm.

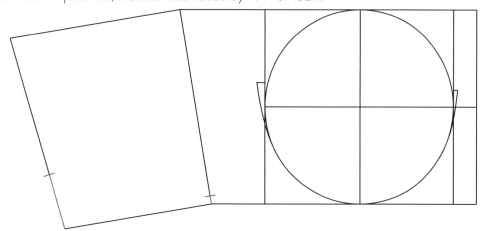

19. At the bottom of the circle, measure down 3/8" or .95cm. This too can be modified depending on how much of a band you desire. 3/8" or .95cm is the minimum amount of room to stitch down the underwire channeling.

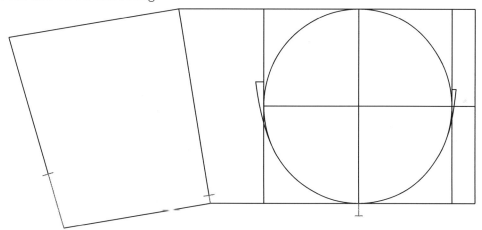

20. At the center front hem, measure an amount of 1/4" to 3/4" or .6cm to 1.9cm This amount is variable based on your design and helps in shaping and comfort. This example was raised 1/2" or 1.25cm.

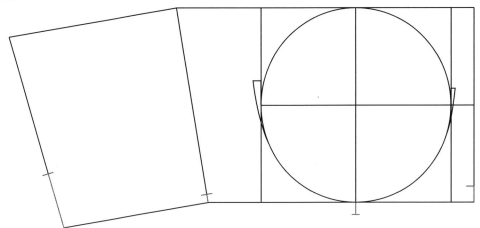

21. Using your hip curve, use a series of curved shapes to shape your hemline, connecting each of the points we marked.

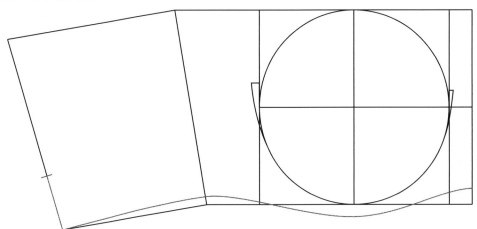

22. a. At the center front curve for the wire, extend the line up 1/2" or 1.25cm. This is to allow for sewing room and ease at the top of the underwire.

   b. At the side of the curve for the wire, extend the line up 1/2" or 1.25cm. Based on your design specs, these amounts could be modified.

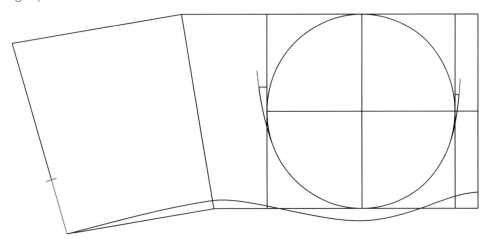

23. Draw a line straight across the center front from the raised marking.

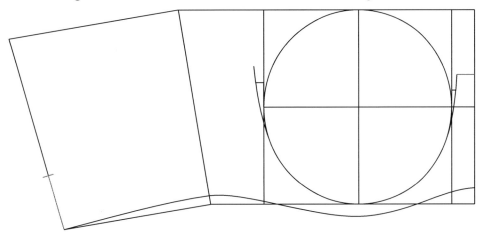

24. At the side seam, measure up from the curve, the same height that is at the center front.

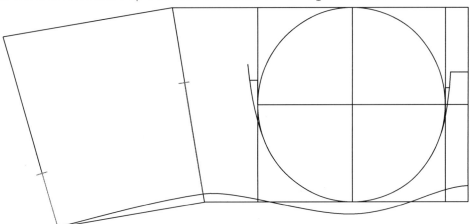

25. a. On the back, fine the absolute center between the side seam and center back. Draw in a temporary guideline. You can find this easily by folding the paper to make the center back and side seam match.

   b. From the curve on that line, measure up the same height as the side seam, this will indicate the strap placement.

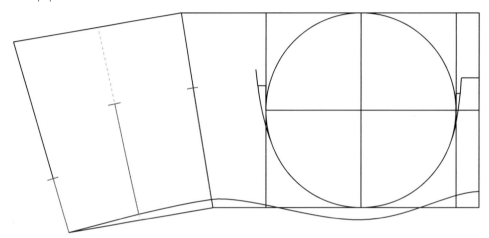

26. Using your hip curve and french curve, blend in the back and front band shape as pictured.

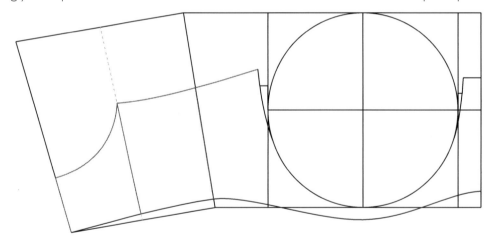

CHAPTER 16

BRA CUP
PATTERN DRAFTING

In this chapter, we will draft a two piece cup. These directions can easily be adapted for a three piece cup using this chapter in conjunction with Chapter 3.

TWO PIECE BRA CUP

1. Begin by drawing intersecting lines through your paper. From the center point, measure down the radius of the bust or half the diameter.

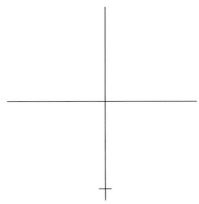

2. Use a compass to draw the circumference around the center point.

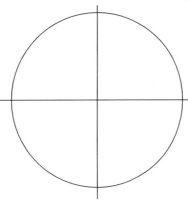

3. Cut the circle in half. Take the top half and label top cup and the lower half, lower cup.

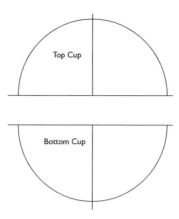

4. A breast is not a perfect circle nor is it symmetrical, so we need to increase the width of the cup based on two factors.

    a. The first is an assumption that the diameter of the breast tissue is wider than the height diameter. This will vary based on individual and size. Based on measuring several different women, this diameter difference varied from 1" to 2" or 2.5cm to 5cm. For these directions, I will be using the average measurement which is 1-1/2" or 3.8cm.

Average Width Increase	1-1/2" or 3.8cm

If you have the option to get up close and personal with your subject, place the underwire that corresponds to their measurements under the bust and measure across the bust from wire end to end. Whatever the width is, subtract the height from it.

	Left Bust	Right Bust
Height Diameter of Bust		
Width Diameter of Bust		
Difference of Measurements		

The center of the bust cup will be increased by one of these two amounts.

    b. The difference of measurements between the under bust and chest measurements. Since we are working on one quarter of the body, refer to the quarter measurements of the body.

1/4 Chest Measurement	
1/4 Under Bust Measurement	
Difference	

5. Start with the lower cup. Cut down the center towards the lower curve. Do not cut through. Separate the top portion by the distance determined in step 4.a. (for the diameter change).

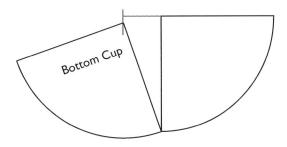

6. The cup must fit into the circumference of the wire. Refer to page 125, step 1 for the wire diameters used in the band draft. Calculate the circumference of the wire by multiplying the wire diameter by Pi (3.141592). Divide that number by 4, to separate the cup into 4 pieces.

	Left Bust	Right Bust
Wire measurement		
Multiply by 3.141592		
Divide by 4		

LOWER CUP

7. Take the 1/4 amount from 6 above and measure up the sides of the curve from the center point. Use a flexible ruler to get an accurate measurement.

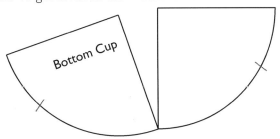

8. Draw a line from the marking to the slashed corner of each side.

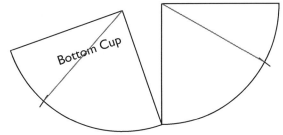

9. Based on the diameter of the bust, use the following chart to determine how much shaping is needed for inner curves of the cup. This is based on 5% of the diameter of the cup. When you test the fit of your custom bras, you may wish to alter this amount if the breast is not filling the cup thoroughly.

IMPERIAL MEASUREMENTS

Diameter	5% Amount	Diameter	5% Amount
5	1/8	12	5/16
5 1/2	1/8	12 1/2	5/16
6	1/8	13	5/16
6 1/2	3/16	13 1/2	5/16
7	3/16	14	3/8
7 1/2	3/16	14 1/2	3/8
8	3/16	15	3/8
8 1/2	3/16	15 1/2	3/8
9	1/4	16	3/8
9 1/2	1/4	16 1/2	7/16
10	1/4	17	7/16
10 1/2	1/4	17 1/2	7/16
11	1/4	18	7/16
11 1/2	5/16		

METRIC MEASUREMENTS

Diameter	5% Amount	Diameter	5% Amount
12.5	0.3	30	0.8
13.75	0.3	31.25	0.8
15	0.4	32.5	0.8
16.25	0.4	33.75	0.8
17.5	0.4	35	0.9
18.75	0.5	36.25	0.9
20	0.5	37.5	0.9
21.25	0.5	38.75	1.0
22.5	0.6	40	1.0
23.75	0.6	41.25	1.0
25	0.6	42.5	1.1
26.25	0.7	43.75	1.1
27.5	0.7	45	1.1
28.75	0.7		

10. Find the mid point on the straight lines for each piece. On both sides measure out the 5% amount.

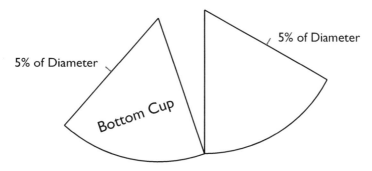

5% of Diameter

5% of Diameter

Bottom Cup

11. a. At the top of the right pie shape, measure down 1/2" or 1.25cm on the center line. This is to remove the steep curve which can cause a pointed apex. This amount can be varied based on your preference of fit.

   b. Since we are removing 1/2" or 1.25cm from the top, we need to add it to the bottom in order to keep the volume of the cup consistent. Changing the volume of the cup will cause difficulties in fit because these patterns are based on bust volume. (Alter this amount to match the amount you are removing from the top.)

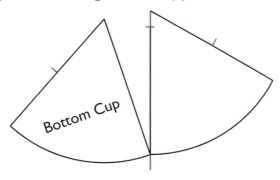

Bottom Cup

12. a. Create a smooth curve at the top of the cup by connecting the lower points, the 5% amounts and the lowered amount from step 11.a. If your curve doesn't quite meet each point, don't worry, they are only guidelines to assist in shaping.

   b. On the lower portion of the cup, blend out a smooth curve connecting the side points to the lowered point.

   c. Add notches at the positions indicated in the illustration . The top marks the apex and the bottom indicates the center cup.

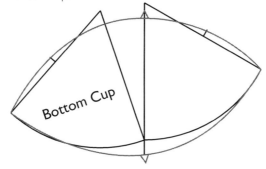

Bottom Cup

TOP CUP

13. a. Take the top cup and cut it in half on the center line. Separate the lower part of the cup by the amount from step 4.a.

   b. At the top of the cup, we also need to add in the width change of the body from step 4.b. Separate the upper part by 4.a. + 4.b.

		Standard Imperial	Standard Metric	Custom Left	Custom Right
#4.a.	Cup Width Increase	1-1/2"	3.75cm		
#4.b.	Chest Difference	1"	2.5cm		
	Total	2-1/2"	6.25cm		

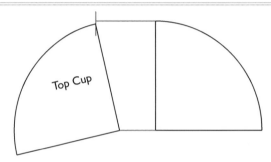

14. Take the 1/4 measurement from step 6 and mark on the curve from the top down.

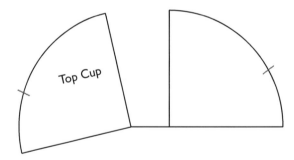

15. Draw a line from the left marking towards the right center line. On the right side, draw a line from the right marking to the same line.

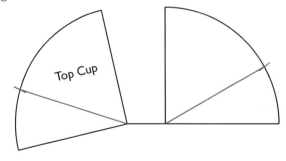

16. Find the center of both straight lines and measure out 5% from the chart on page 140 based on the bust diameter.

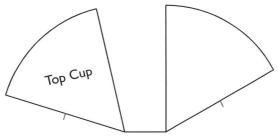

17. a. On the right side, use the hip curve to connect the upper right point, the 5% amount and the tip of the right pie shape. Use the curved side of the hip curve at the pie tips.

    b. On the left side, use the hip curve to connect the upper left point, the 5% point and both the pie tips. The cup should be off center. Place a temporary notch at the right pie tip.

    c. At the top, smooth a curve connecting the two pie pieces.

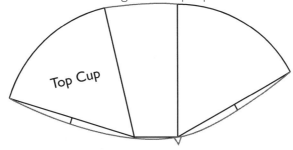

18. Take the two cups and walk the length of the center seam together, starting at the center notch and moving outwards. These lines will most likely be different on one or both sides. Find the center point between the shorter and longer seam. This is called balancing a seam length. Repeat this on both sides. Connect the new markings to the existing curve.

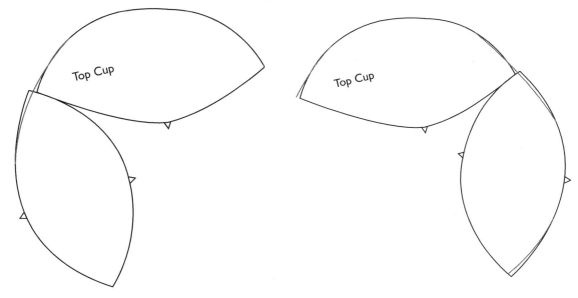

19. We need to walk the new cup edges into the band curve. Start on the lower cup at the center point notch. Walk the cup into the original circle from the band draft. At both sides, you will notice the wire curve, mark on your cup where the new line is when your cup is lined up to the old circle.

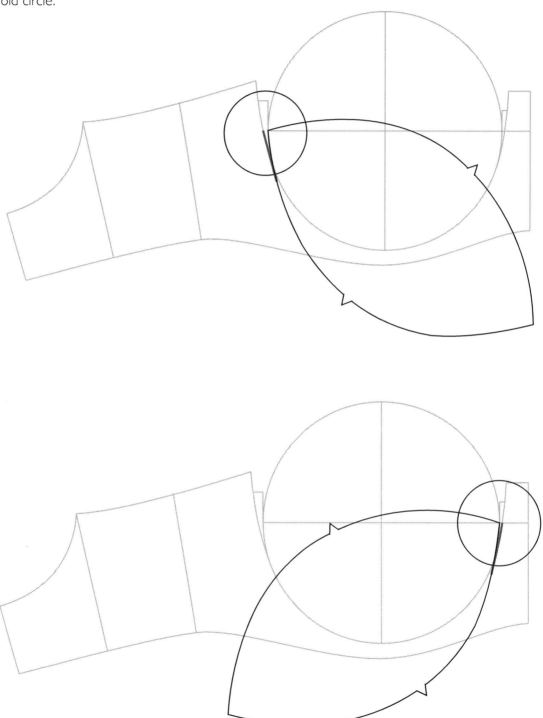

20. The upper cup will be done in a similar manner. Start the upper cup walking on the original circle. Mark where the new line is from the band curve. Also mark where the band curve ends. Repeat this on both sides.

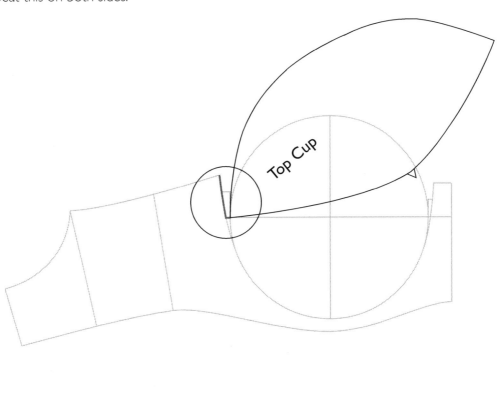

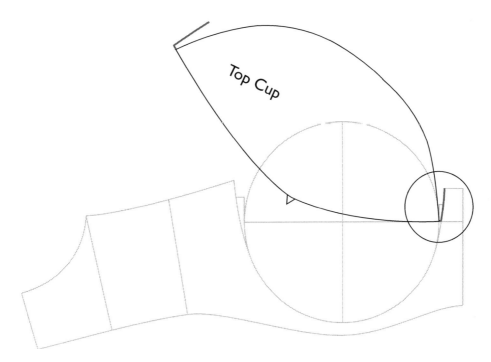

21. On the upper cup, we need to determine the strap placement. The strap should be about 1/4 of the distance across the cup. To easily determine this point, fold the cup matching the CF and SS. Fold again to make it quarters.

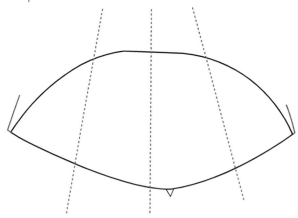

22. At the left first quarter, mark up about 1" or 2.5cm up on the fold from the curve. Square a line across 1/2" or 1.25cm to the right. These amount can vary based on your design and strap width. This is for a 1/2" or 1.25cm strap.

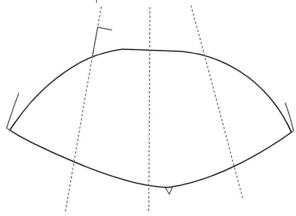

23. Use the hip curve to shape the underarm in a fairly deep curve and shape the neckline with a mild curve from the center to the strap. Both of these lines can vary depending on your design specifications.

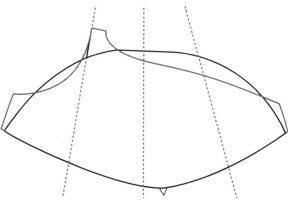

CHAPTER 17

PATTERN DIRECTIONS

This chapter takes the drafts created in Chapter 15 and 16 and prepares them as patterns for cutting and construction.

BRA BAND

When creating the pattern for your bra, there are a few variables to consider. How do you plan to attach your elastics and finish your edges? These decisions can affect the seam lines and allowance. The following steps follow the construction methods from Chapter 2. For variations of elastic attachments, refer to the changes made in Chapters 3 and 4 to modify these directions for different elastics.

1. Begin by noting the style lines on the band. Make sure you have the back strap placement indicated if you have modified the back band shape.

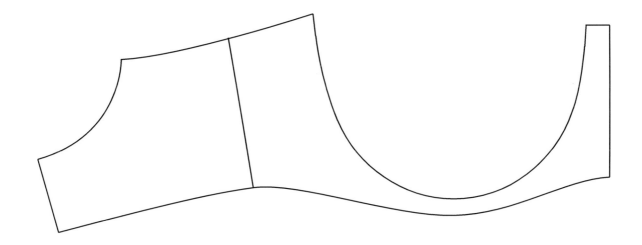

2. Separate the front and back pattern pieces.

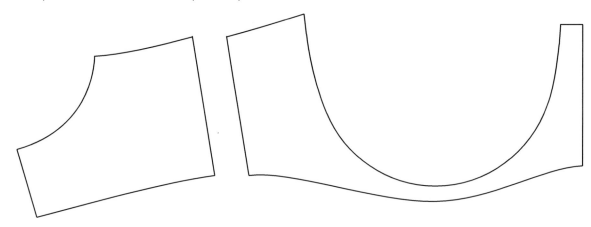

3. Add 1/4" or .6cm seam allowance around all edges except the center front which will be cut on the fold. You can either cut your front cup on the fold or cut two, leaving a seam at the center front (cutting two would require seam allowance at the center front).

BRA CUP

4. Trace off your basic cup patterns.

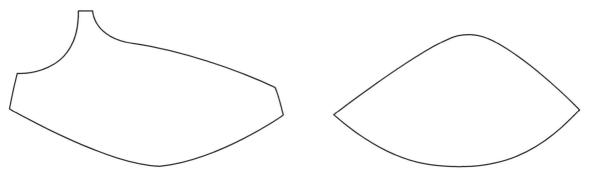

5. Around the outside curve and neckline, your seam allowance is 1/4" or .6cm.

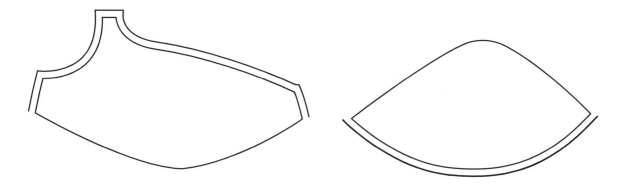

6. Interior seam lines can have a seam allowance of 1/8" or 1/4" (.3cm or .6cm). In manufacturing, the interior seam allowance will often be 1/8" or .3cm. For most custom clothiers, a seam allowance of 1/4" or .6cm is more practical.

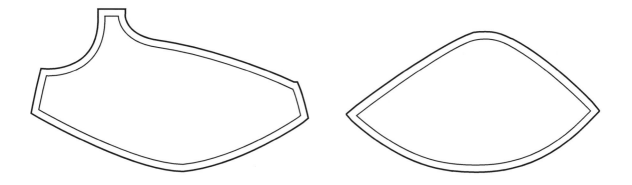

LABELING

The last step in creating your patterns is to add grainlines and pertinent pattern information. Pattern information should include the style name and/or number, piece name, size and cutting instructions.

7. On the back band, line up the grainline to the side seam.

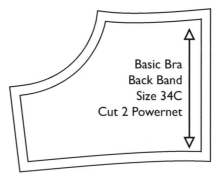

Basic Bra
Back Band
Size 34C
Cut 2 Powernet

8. On the front band, line up the grainline to the center front.

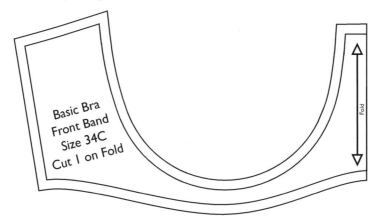

Basic Bra
Front Band
Size 34C
Cut 1 on Fold

Fold

9. On the cup pieces, the grainline can vary. For the sake of these steps, place the grainline straight through the center of the cups. For variations, change the grainline and test the fit. Each movement of the grainline will vary the way the cup fits.

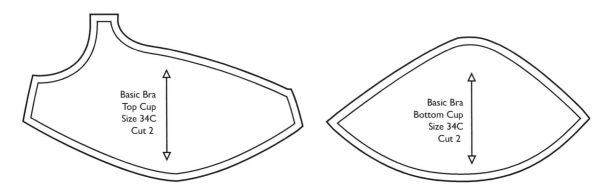

Basic Bra
Top Cup
Size 34C
Cut 2

Basic Bra
Bottom Cup
Size 34C
Cut 2

CHAPTER 18

BRA BAND GRADING

Grading for bras are more complicated than grading for any other garment. Bras are graded in two parts. First by grading the band for different cup sizes and second by grading a cup size for different band sizes.

GRADING FOR CUP SIZES

BAND FRONT

1. Begin with your front band draft. Trace off all the lines indicated below.

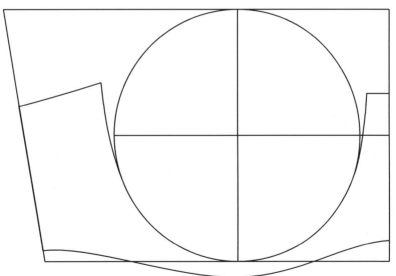

2. Vertical Guides

    a. Draw a vertical line at the left side of the cup curve. This indicates the full grade.

    b. The center line of the cup will indicate half the grade.

    c. Draw a vertical line at the right side of the cup curve. This indicates the zero grade.

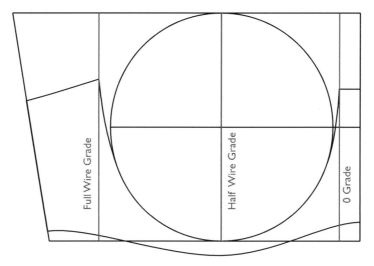

3. Horizontal Guides

    a. Referring to the draft of the band, the top of the wires end based on the center horizontal line of the cup, the height will change by the half grade amount in the height. Make a horizontal guide at the top of the wires.

    b. The height will also change based on the wire diameter. Place a horizontal guide at the top. This will represent a full cup grade.

    c. The lowest horizontal line marks the zero grade.

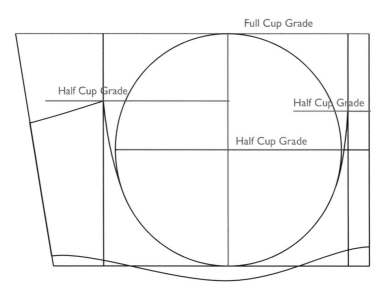

3. The cup size grade is based on the wire sizes. The following table represents a general cup grade. This may differ for different wire manufacturer.

	Imperial	Metric	Custom
Full Cup Grade	5/16 "(.31)	.79cm	
Half Cup Grade	5/32" (.15625)	.39cm	

4. Because the height of the center front changes in grade, and the side seam is set to be the same height as the center front, we will need to adjust the side seam. Draw a perpendicular guideline at the top of the side seam.

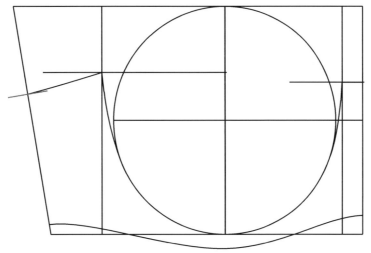

5. Start by drawing in the center cup half grade change of one size. In this example, the grade decreases by one size.

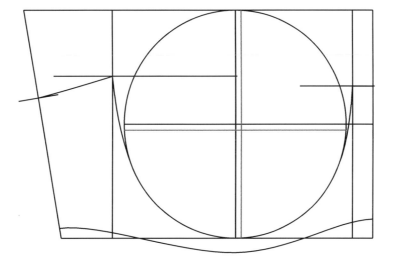

6. Take your compass and draw in a circle using the new center point at the tip of the compass and the pencil line at the lower horizontal line.

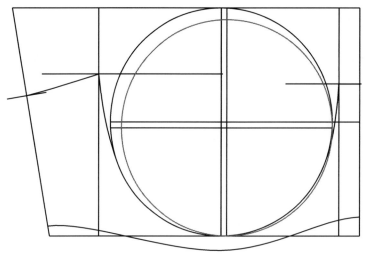

7. a. At the top of the wire at the center front, draw in your new height which is the half grade amount. Blend a curve from the lower half of the circle up to the new top of wire. This line will be very close to the existing line, but will vary slightly.

    b. On the left side of the wire, draw in your new height (half grade).

    c. The left side of the cup also changes in width by the full grade. Mark this position and blend a curve from the lower half of the circle up to this point.

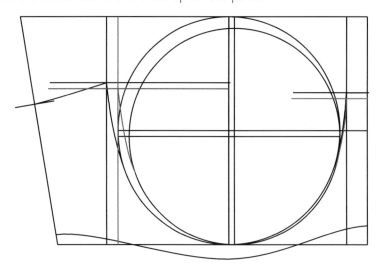

8. a. At the side seam, the height is altered by the half grade. Draw in the new height guide line.

   b. At the top of the cup, draw a parallel line to the top the exact length, but lowered at the full cup grade. This line should touch the top of the new circle.

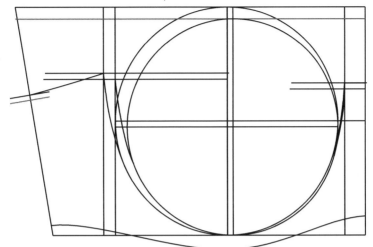

9. a. Draw in the new side seam from the top of the new horizontal line down the base of the line.

   b. Draw in your new underarm curve from the side seam to the wire side.

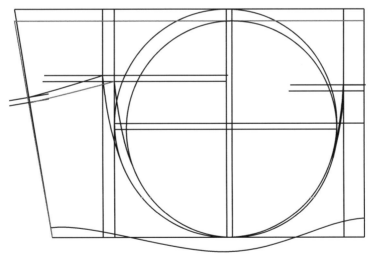

BACK BAND

10. Trace off the back band and add the following horizontal guidelines. Place one at the top of the side seam and one at the top of the strap, both perpendicular to the height line.

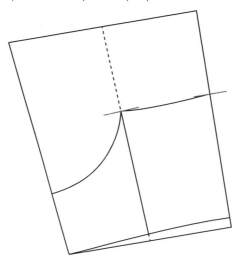

11. The center back may increase or decrease in size but it varies based on the number of hook & eyes you wish to place on the back. For this example, we will decrease the center back by 1/2" or 1.25cm for one less row of hooks & eyes. See the table on page 132 to determine the hook & eye row measurements.

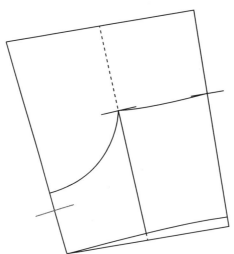

12. Decrease the height of the strap and side seam by the half grade amount.

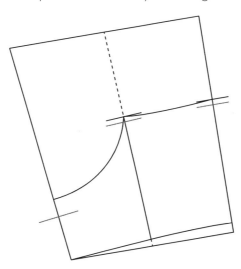

13. a. At the top of the back, draw a parallel line to the top the exact length, but lowered at the full cup grade.

   b. Draw in the new side seam from the top of the new horizontal line down the base of the line.

   c. Draw in your new neckline curve from the center back to the side seam. Match this line up to the front to make sure you have a smooth curve.

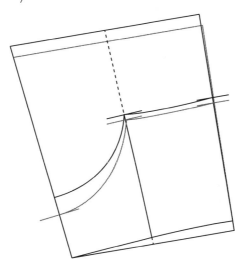

GRADING FOR BAND SIZES

The difference in these directions is that we will be grading the band size for the same wire. This means that each variation of band will be a different cup size.

For example, a 34C graded to a 36 would be a 36B and graded to a 32 band would be a 32D; all of which use the same wire. Refer to the charts on pages 22 to 25 to fully understand how wire sizes change across band sizes. Once you have established a range of band sizes, you can grade each band for the separate cup/wire sizes.

1. Start with your band draft. Trace off your front and back separately and trace all the lines indicated below.

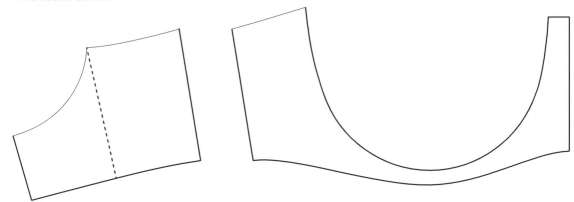

2. You will need two different sets of grade rules. One for the front (for a non stretch grade) and one for the back (for the stretch grade). Look at the grade for 1/4 of the body for both the front and back. On the back, the half grade amount is also needed for strap placement. In this example, our stretch multiplier is .75 for power net. Customize your back grade to correspond to the fabric you are using.

FRONT GRADE SPLIT		
Front Grade	1/2" or 1.25cm	
BACK GRADE SPLIT		
	Standard	Custom
Stretch Multiplier	.75	
Back Grade	3/8" or .95cm	
Half grade	3/16" or .475cm	

For these grading rules, there are only three places for adjustments: the front side seam, the back side seam and the back strap position.

3. On the front, adjust the side seam by the front grade. Keep the height of the line the same, so square a line across from both the top and bottom by 1/2" or 1.25cm.

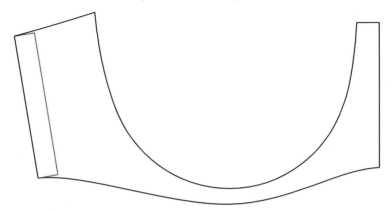

4. Create your new neckline and hem shape connecting to the graded side seam.

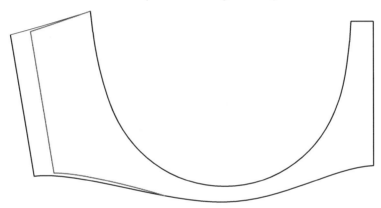

5. On the back, adjust the side seam by the reduced back grade and the strap placement by half the grade amount for the back.

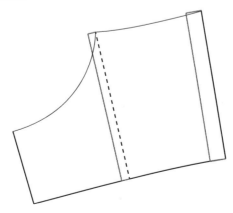

6. Draw in the new neckline and hem shapes for the graded size. Depending on the shape of your hemline, your hem shape may not change.

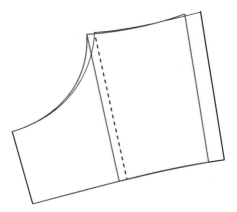

CHAPTER 19

BRA CUP GRADING

Just as the band was grade for both width and girth, the cup must also be graded in the same manner.

GRADING FOR CUP SIZES

1. Draw a line down the center of your paper. Trace the two piece cup you created in Chapter 16, lining up the notch of the top cup and both notches of the bottom cup on this center line. These directions can be adapted for multiple cup pieces by using the same grading principles.

Grading a cup is unlike any other grading. The 0 grade falls at the apex of the cup and the grade radiates from the apex, meaning that the largest graded amount on the cup is a half grade.

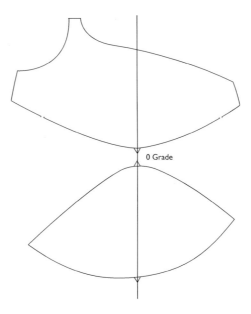

2. For grading a cup, consider the size change for each cup size. The cup sizes change by 1/2" or 1.25cm. The following chart breaks down the grade split. All the following directions will refer to this chart.

	US	UK/Euro	Australia
Full Diameter	1/2"	1.25cm	1cm
Half Cup Grade	1/4"	.62cm	.5cm
1/4 Cup Grade	1/8"	.31cm	.25cm

3. The height of the strap falls into the category of the half grade. Draw a guideline at the top of the strap. In this example we will grade down one size. Mark the half grade amount down on a line parallel to the guideline.

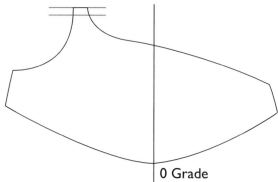

0 Grade

4. On the top cup, the sides of the curve are raised or lowered at 1/4 of the grade. Based on our drafting directions, the length of the side curves on the top cup remain constant. Draw two parallel guides from the points of the curved side at 90 degrees from the curved line. Then draw in a line parallel the amount of the grade change.

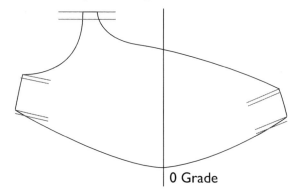

0 Grade

5. Strap placement falls half way between the 0 grade and the 1/2 grade, so the strap placement is at 1/4 grade from the center. Draw in your guide at the strap placement and draw in your new line.

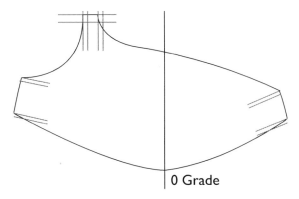

0 Grade

6. The outer curve of the cup is graded at 1/2 of the cup grade. Measure in 1/2 of the grade and create the new cup curves.

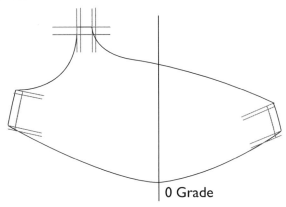

0 Grade

7. Draw in your new top cup shape.

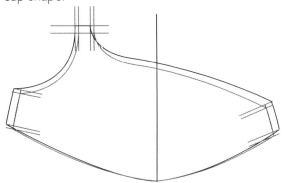

8. On the lower cup, the curved shape that fits into the band increases and decreases in length by the full grade amount of 1/2" or 1.25cm. Because of this, we can't place the same type of guidelines on the lower cup. Place a single guideline perpendicular to the ends of the cup curve.

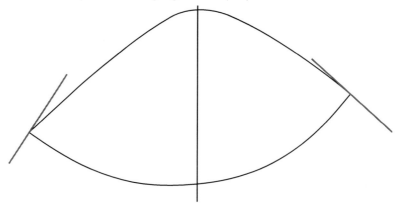

9. On this guideline, mark up or down the half grade amount. Shape in your new size making sure to keep the change at the bottom of the cup at the half grade amount.

Using the flexible ruler, measure the new curve to verify that the length measures exactly the full diameter grade amount. Modify this line to meet this requirement.

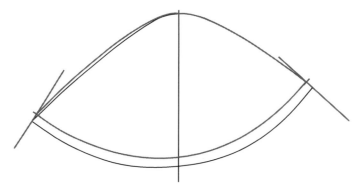

GRADING FOR BAND SIZES

Grading for different band sizes isn't as straight forward as one might think. For these directions, you will be grading a specific diameter for different wire sizes. Refer to the charts on pages 22 through 25 to understand the grade. For example, take a 7" diameter with size 34 band and you have a 34B, but take a 7" diameter for a size 32 band and you have a 32D.

1. The zero grade is at the apex of the cup. The grade change for each wire is 1/2" or 1.25cm. This number is determined by taking the circumference of two wire diameters. The difference is 37/38" or 2.47cm, so to make life less complicated, round up to 1" or 2.5cm. The wire is half of the circumference, so the wire grade is half the circumference grade.

The wire grade needs to be split between all interior joining seams, which equals 1/4 of the wire grade.

	US	UK/Euro	Australia
Circumference Grade	1"	2.5cm	2cm
Wire Grade	1/2"	1.25cm	1cm
Half Wire Grade	1/4"	.62cm	.5cm
Quarter Wire Grade	1/8"	.31cm	.25cm

2. On the interior sides of the top cup, reduce or increase the length of the cup curve by the quarter grade amount.

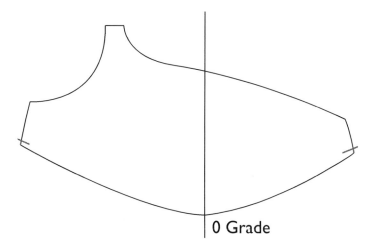

0 Grade

3. Draw in the new curved line and blend to zero at the apex.

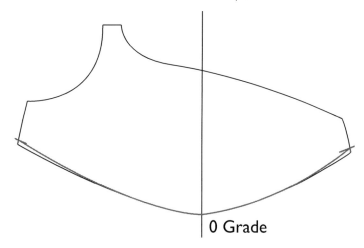

0 Grade

4. At the ends of the lower cup wire curve, shorten or lengthen the outer cup curve by 1/4 of the grade.

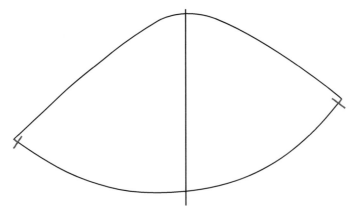

5. Draw in your new lower cup and blend back to zero at the apex. Double check that the seam lengths remain balanced for construction.

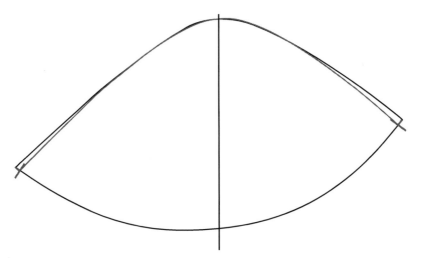

PATTERNS

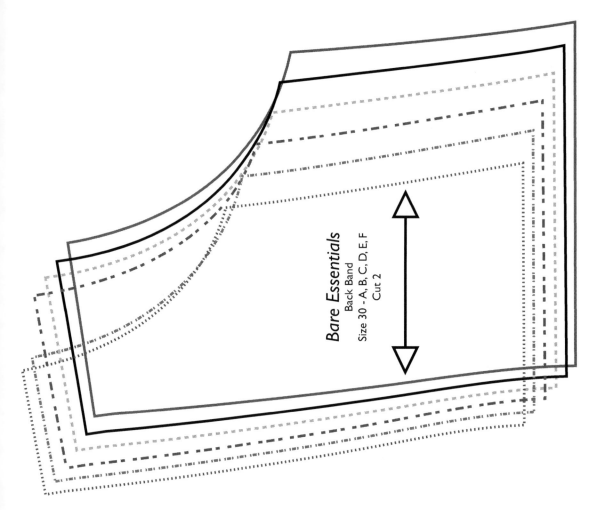

Bare Essentials
Back Band
Size 30 - A, B, C, D, E, F
Cut 2

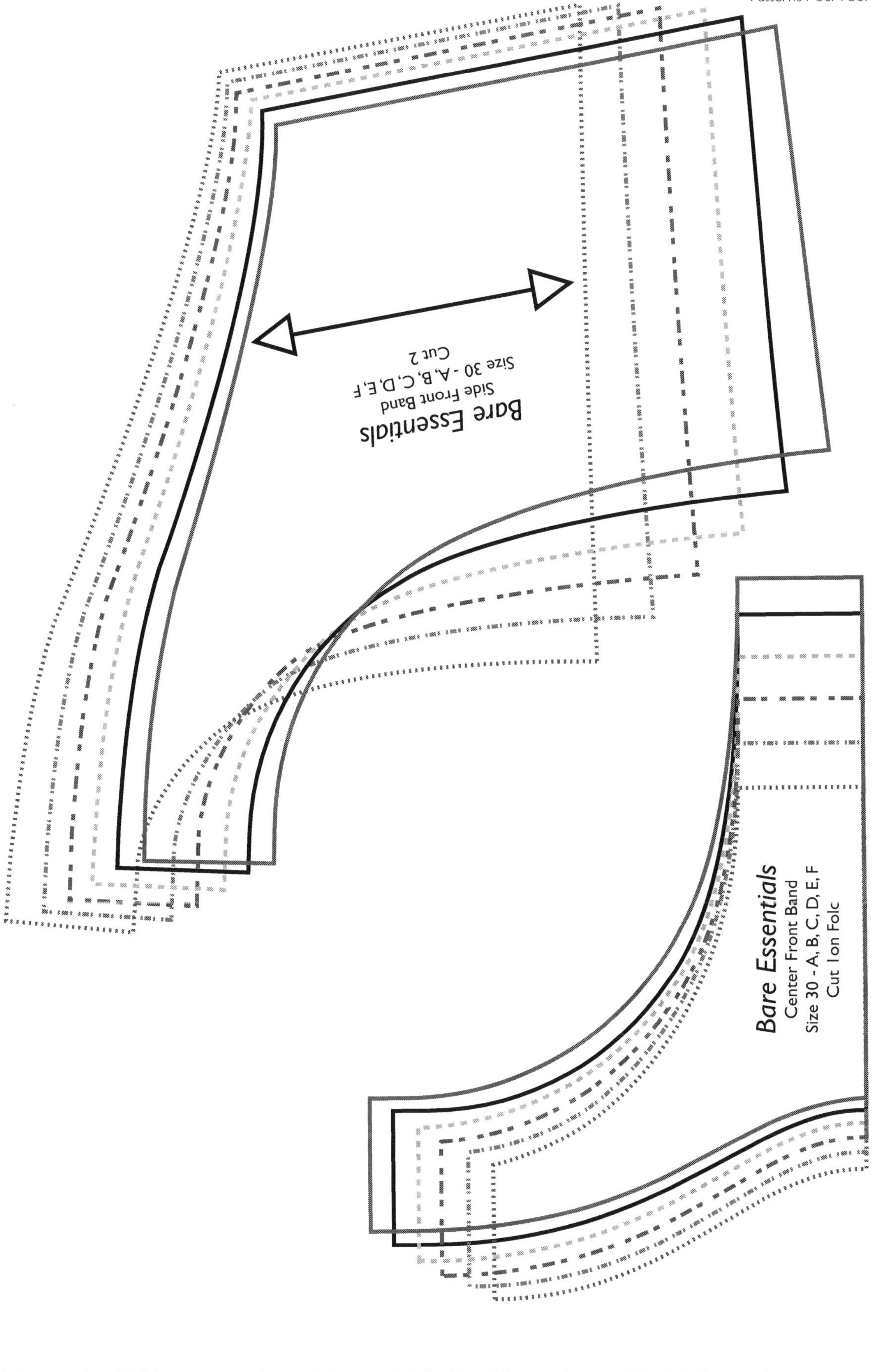

Bare Essentials
Side Front Band
Size 30 - A, B, C, D, E, F
Cut 2

Bare Essentials
Center Front Band
Size 30 - A, B, C, D, E, F
Cut Ion Folc

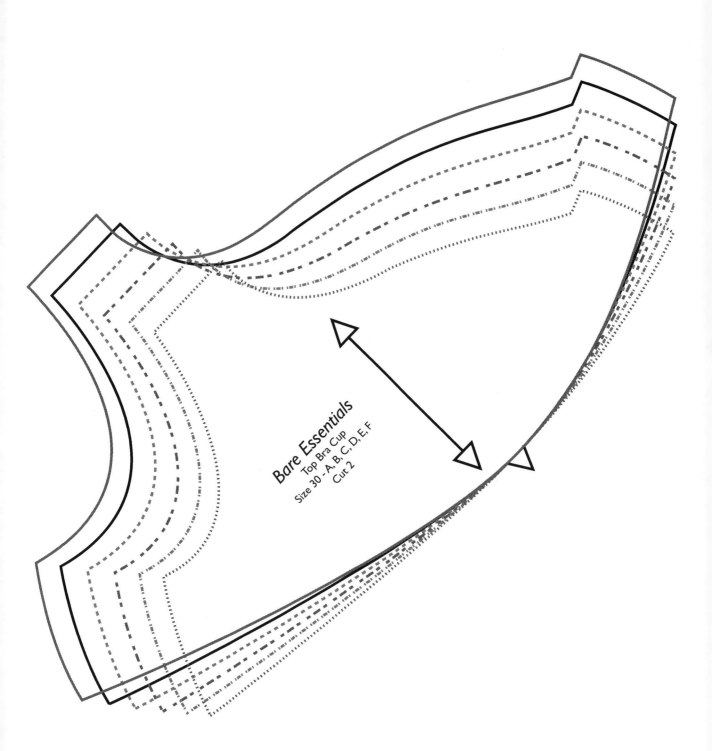

Bare Essentials
Top Bra Cup
Size 30 - A, B, C, D, E, F
Cut 2

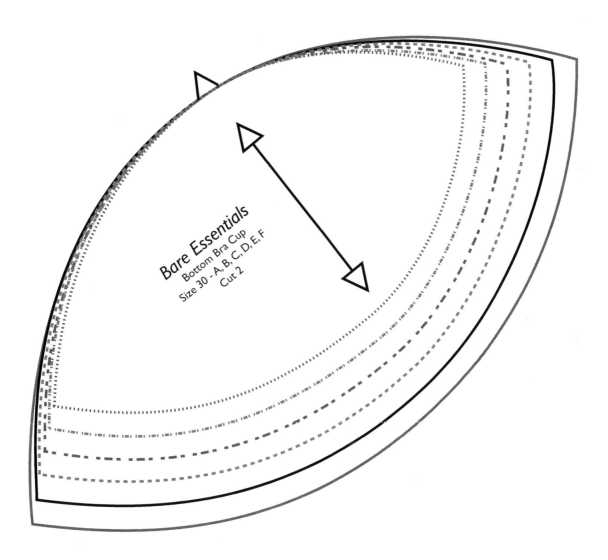

Bare Essentials
Bottom Bra Cup
Size 30 - A, B, C, D, E, F
Cut 2

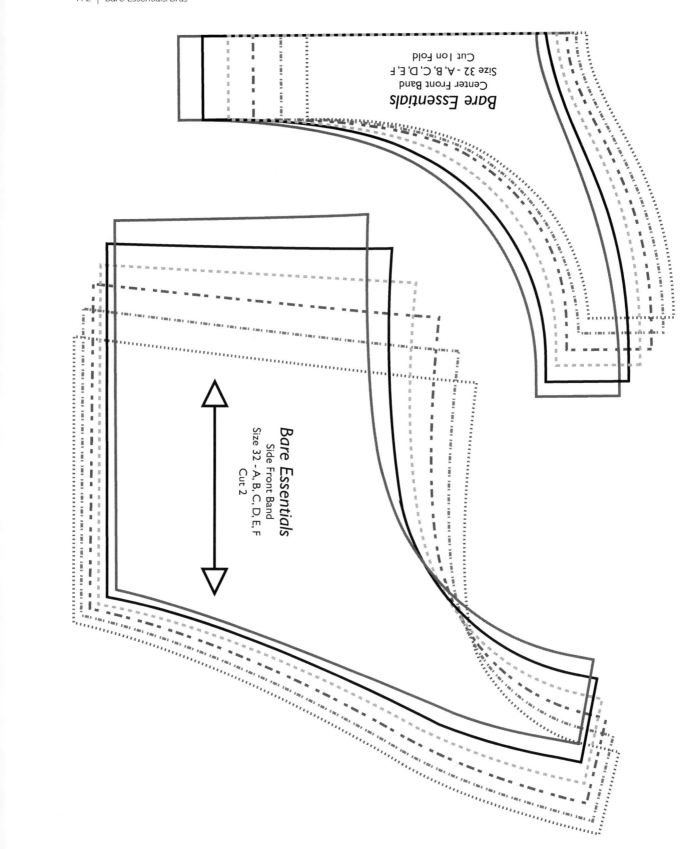

Bare Essentials
Center Front Band
Size 32 - A, B, C, D, E, F
Cut on Fold

Bare Essentials
Side Front Band
Size 32 - A, B, C, D, E, F
Cut 2

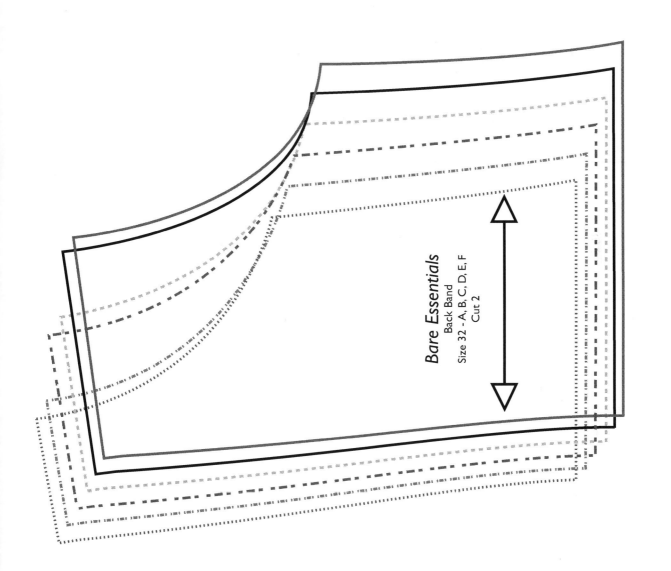

Bare Essentials
Back Band
Size 32 - A, B, C, D, E, F
Cut 2

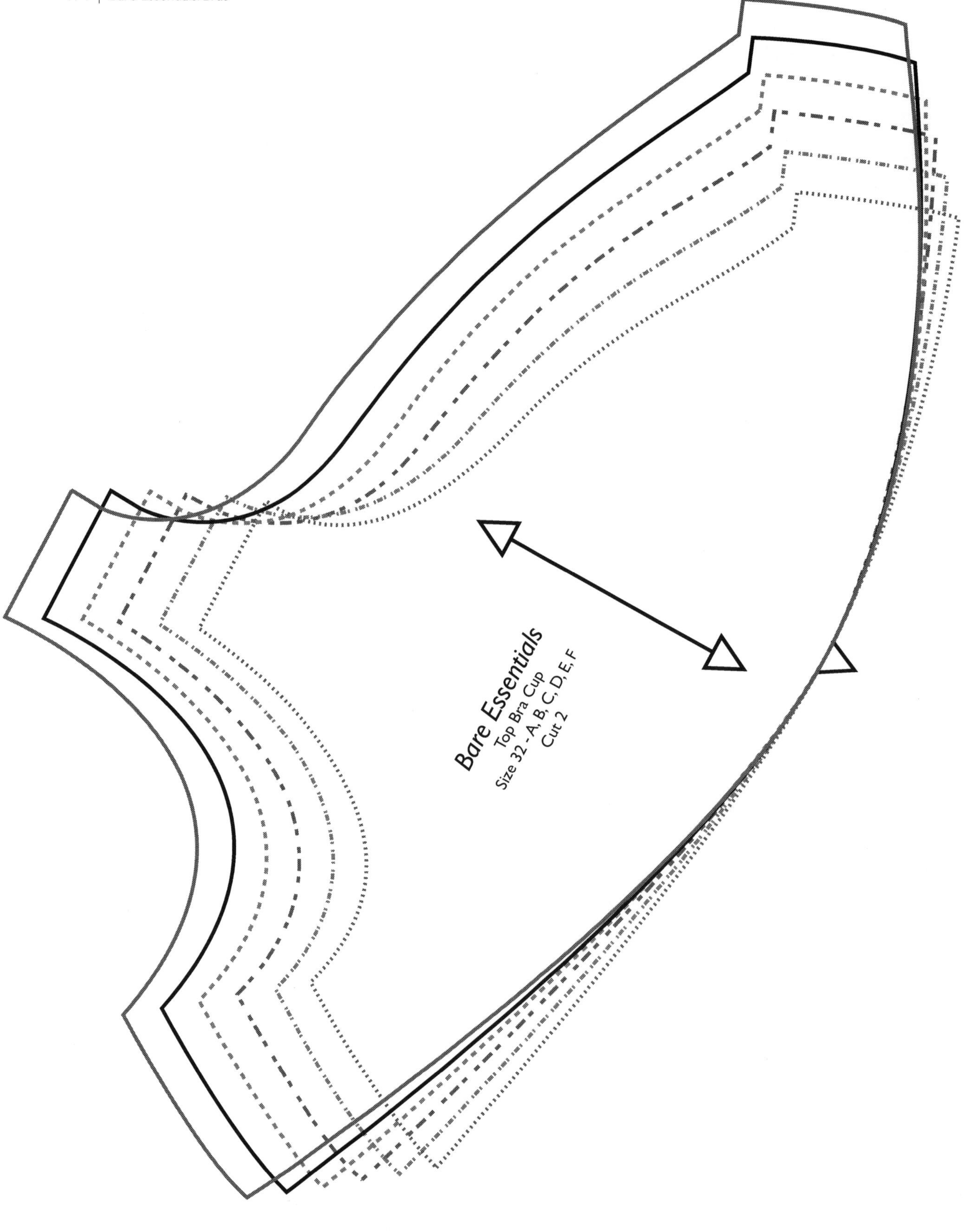

Bare Essentials
Top Bra Cup
Size 32 - A, B, C, D, E, F
Cut 2

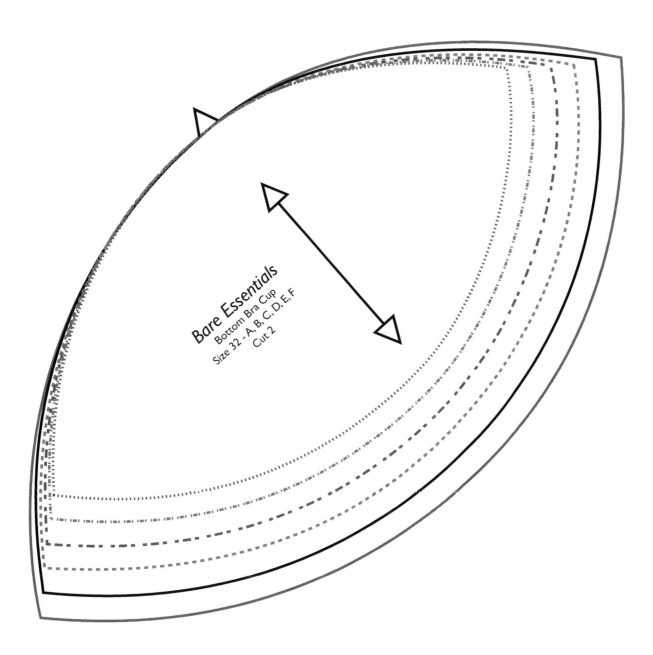

Bare Essentials
Bottom Bra Cup
Size 32 - A, B, C, D, E, F
Cut 2

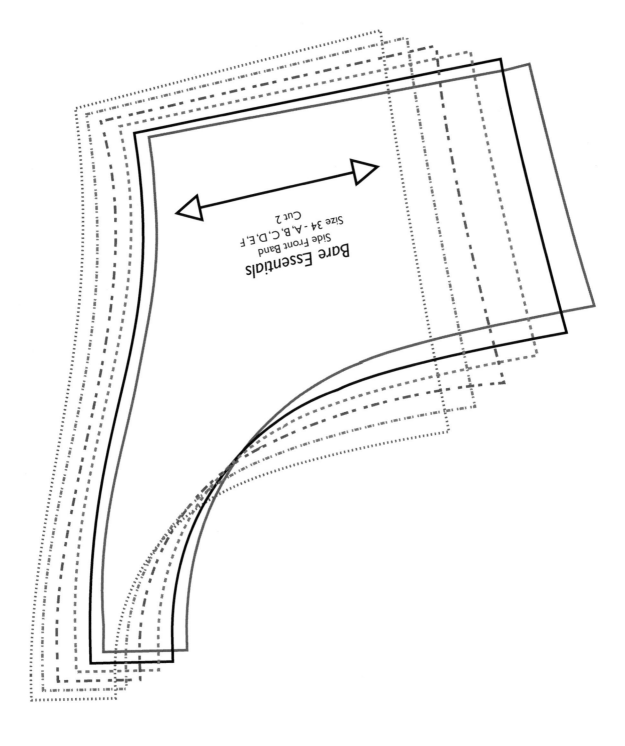

Bare Essentials
Side Front Band
Size 34 - A,B,C,D,E,F
Cut 2

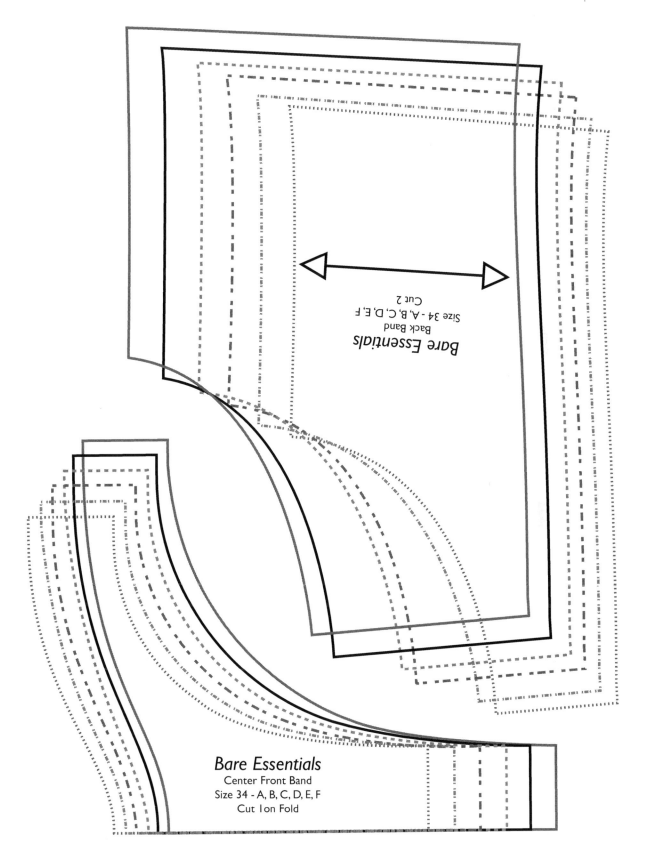

Bare Essentials
Back Band
Size 34 - A, B, C, D, E, F
Cut 2

Bare Essentials
Center Front Band
Size 34 - A, B, C, D, E, F
Cut 1 on Fold

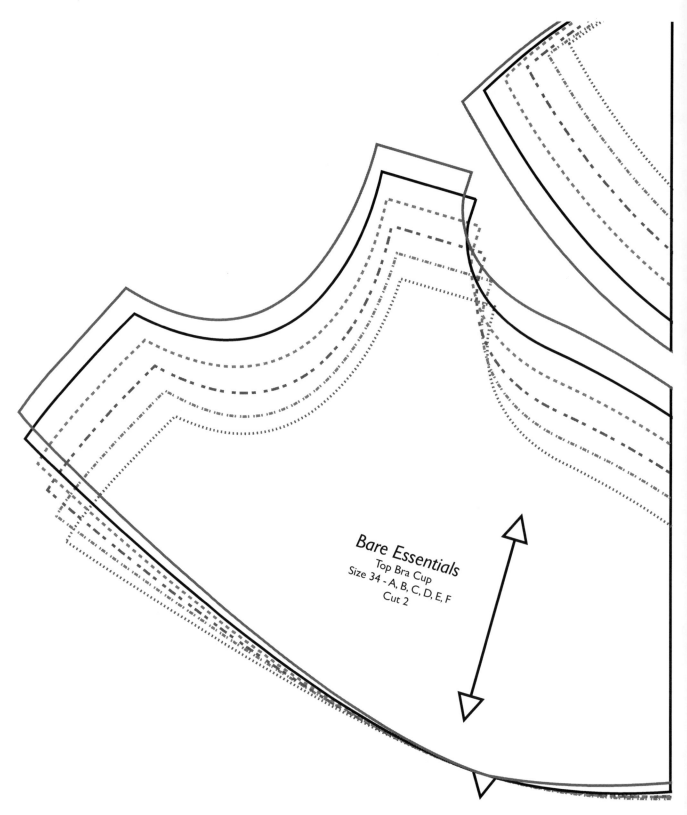

Bare Essentials
Top Bra Cup
Size 34 - A, B, C, D, E, F
Cut 2

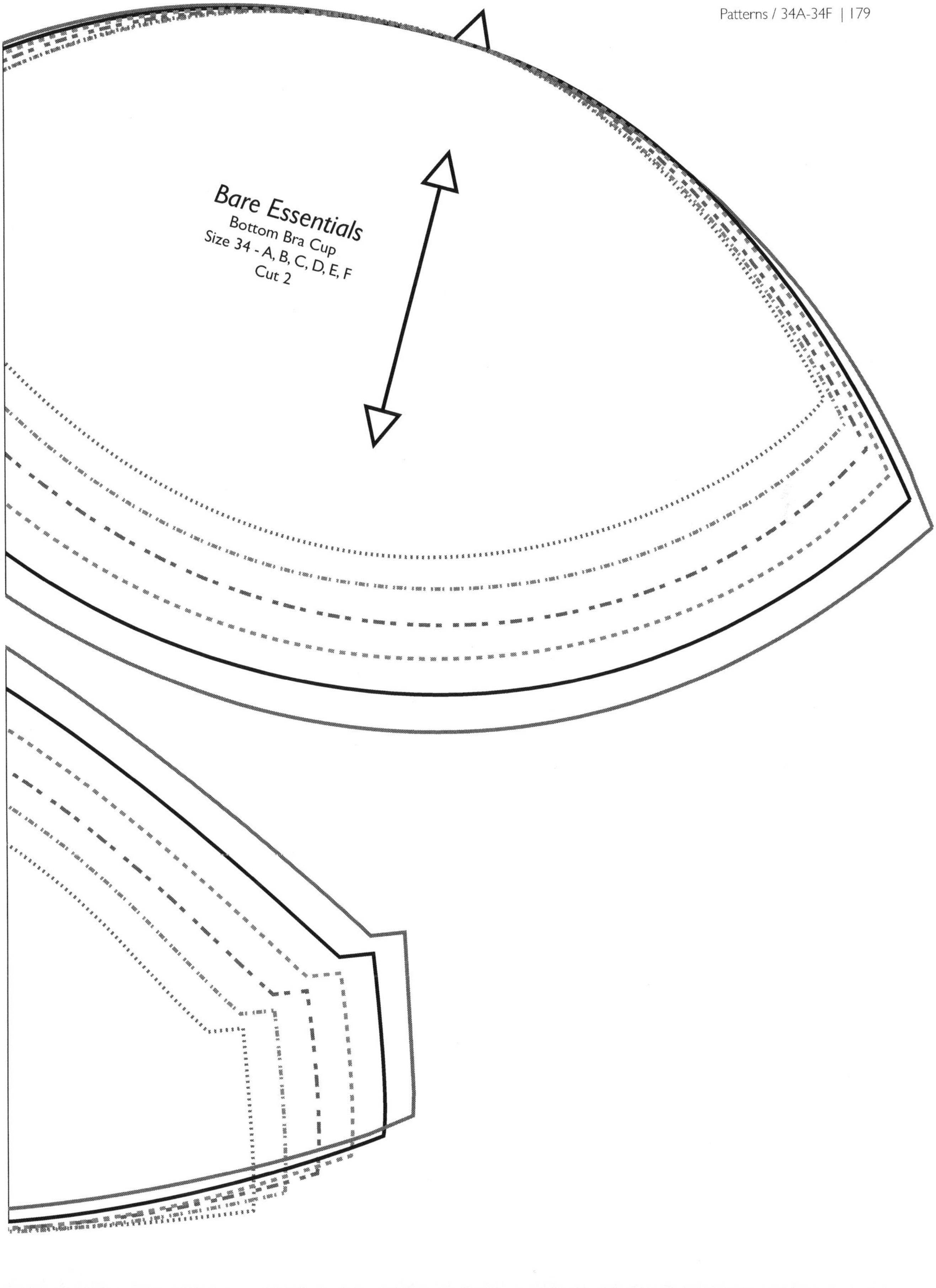

Bare Essentials
Bottom Bra Cup
Size 34 - A, B, C, D, E, F
Cut 2

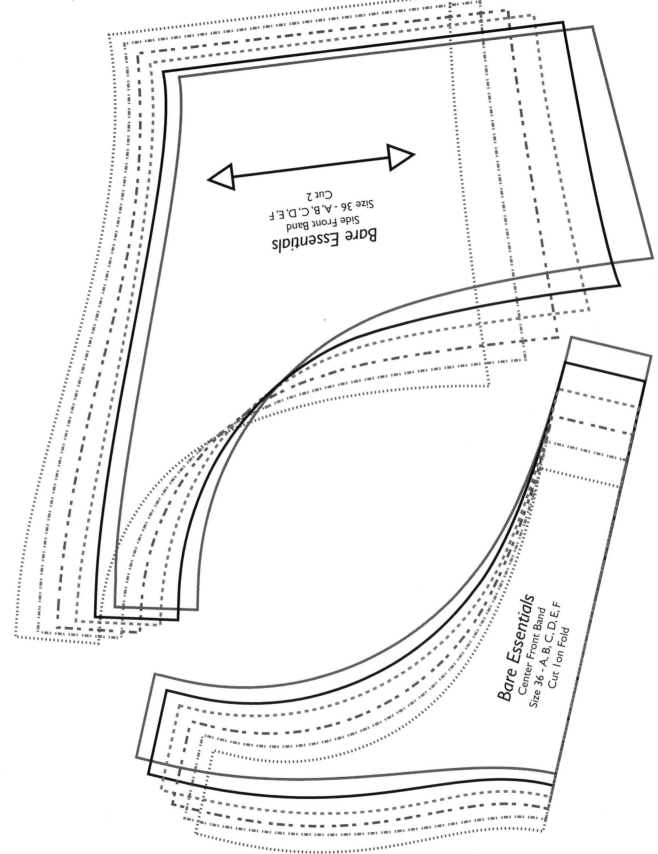

Bare Essentials
Side Front Band
Size 36 - A, B, C, D, E, F
Cut 2

Bare Essentials
Center Front Band
Size 36 - A, B, C, D, E, F
Cut 1 on Fold

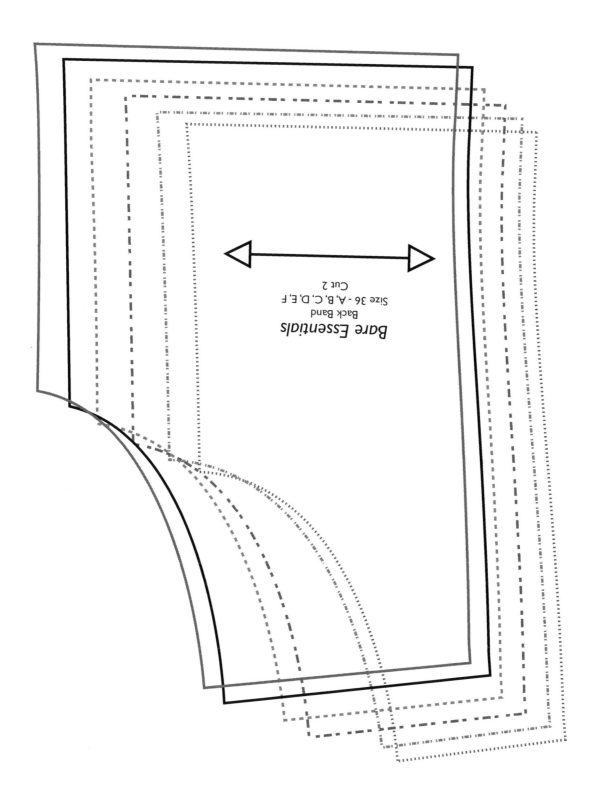

Bare Essentials
Back Band
Size 36 - A, B, C, D, E, F
Cut 2

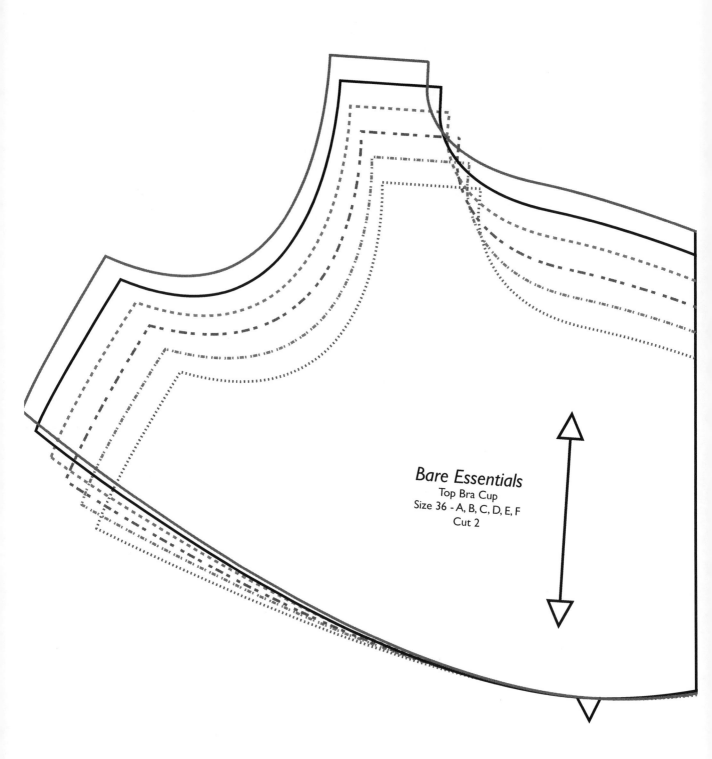

Bare Essentials
Top Bra Cup
Size 36 - A, B, C, D, E, F
Cut 2

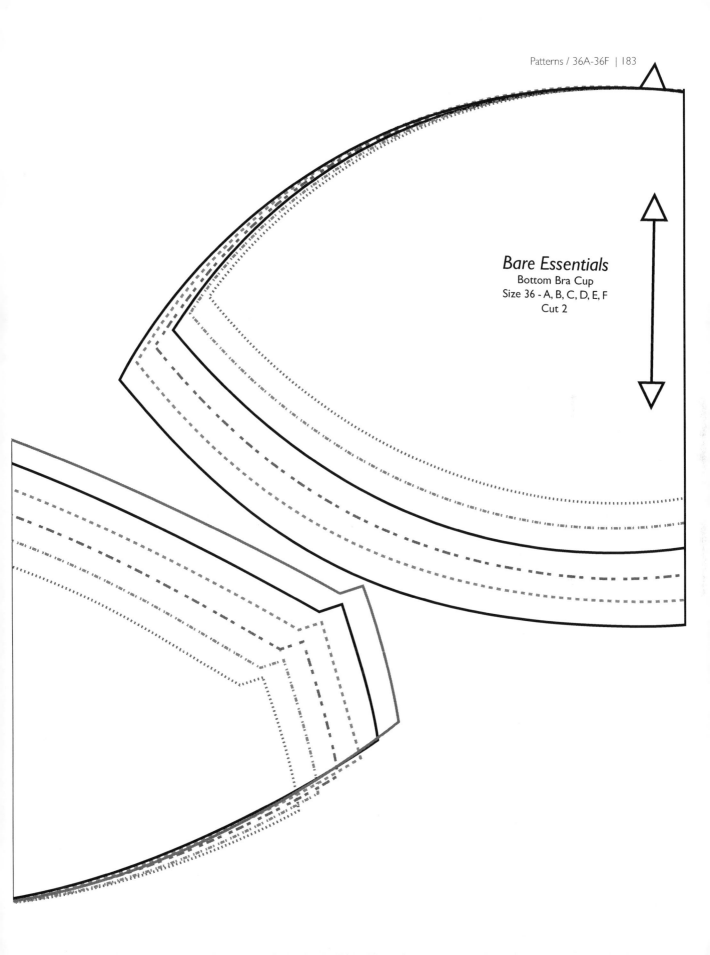

Bare Essentials
Bottom Bra Cup
Size 36 - A, B, C, D, E, F
Cut 2

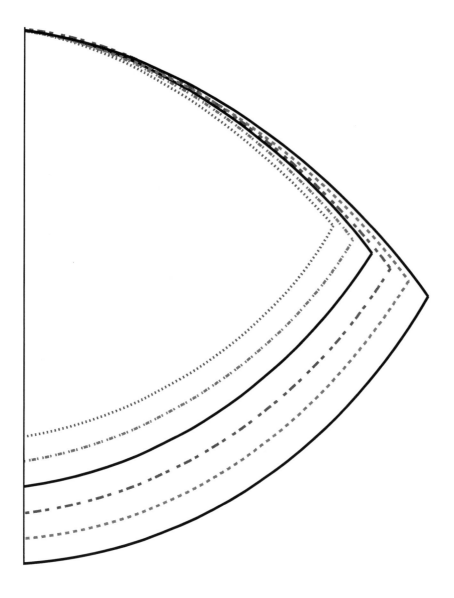

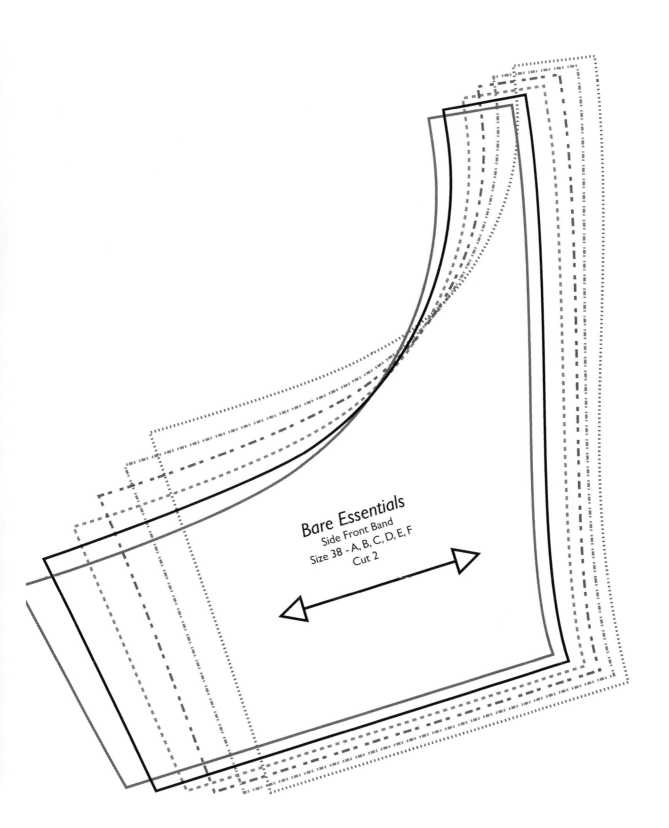

Bare Essentials
Side Front Band
Size 38 - A, B, C, D, E, F
Cut 2

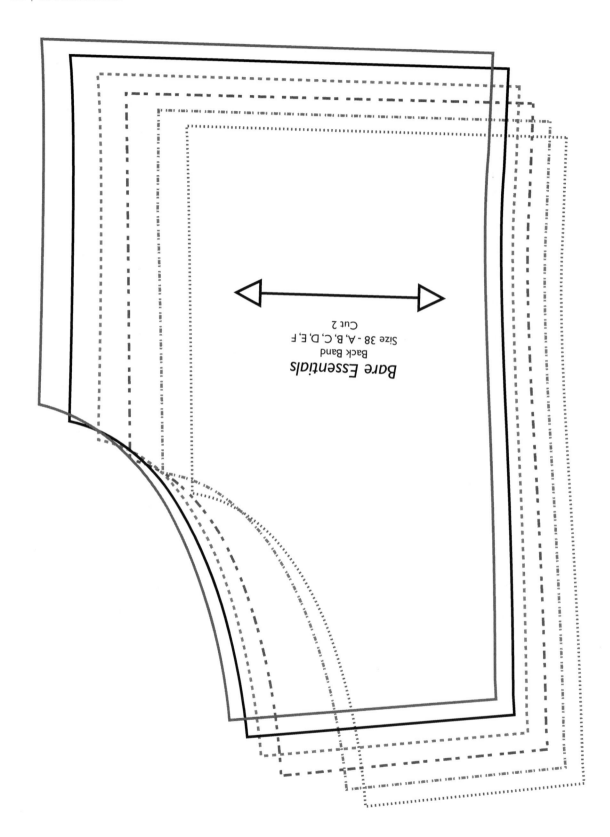

Bare Essentials
Back Band
Size 38 - A, B, C, D, E, F
Cut 2

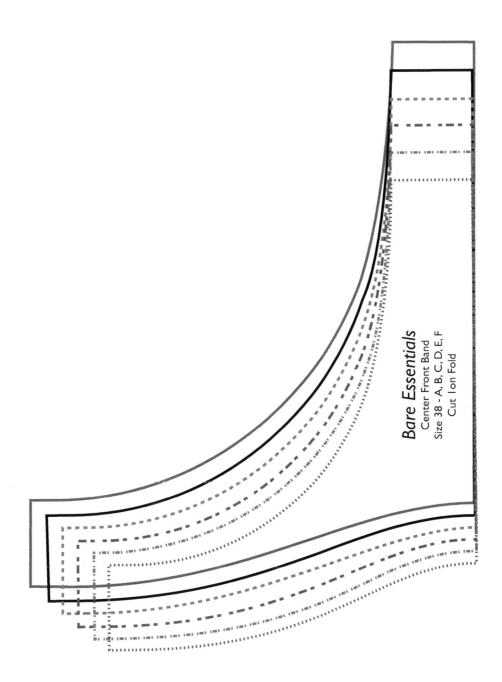

Bare Essentials
Center Front Band
Size 38 - A, B, C, D, E, F
Cut Ion Fold

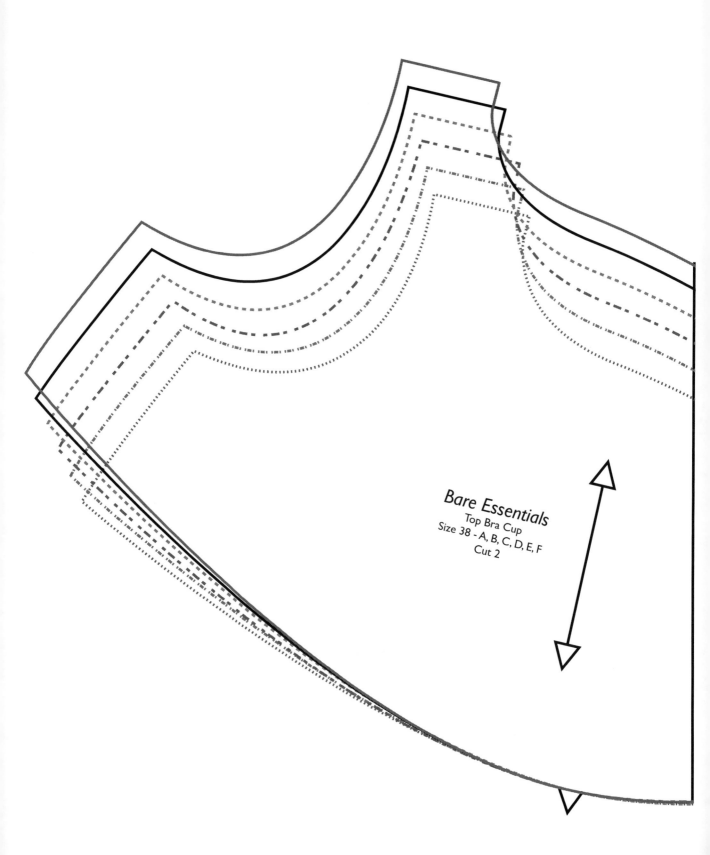

Bare Essentials
Top Bra Cup
Size 38 - A, B, C, D, E, F
Cut 2

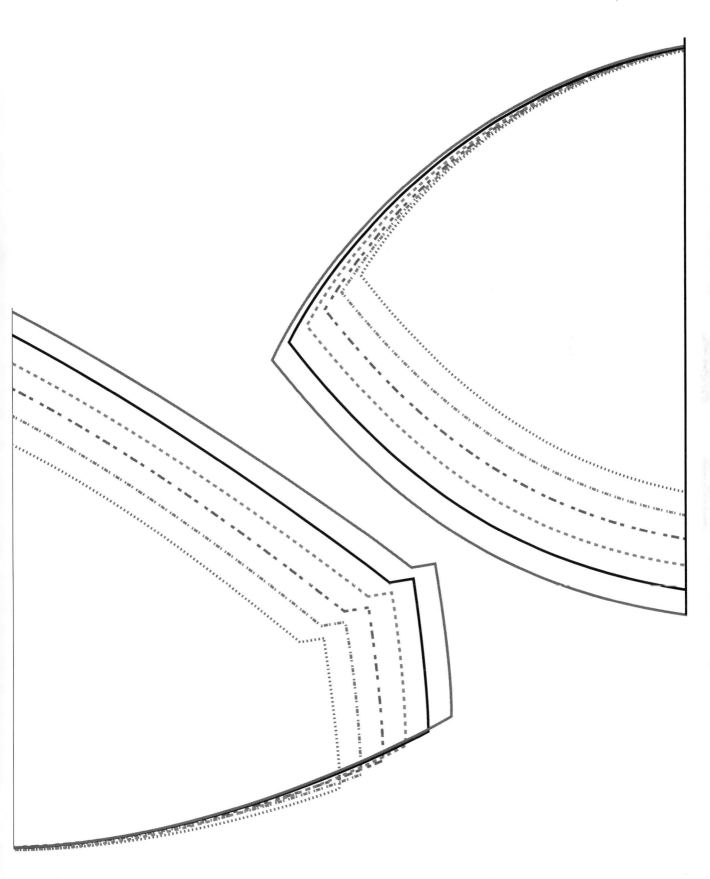

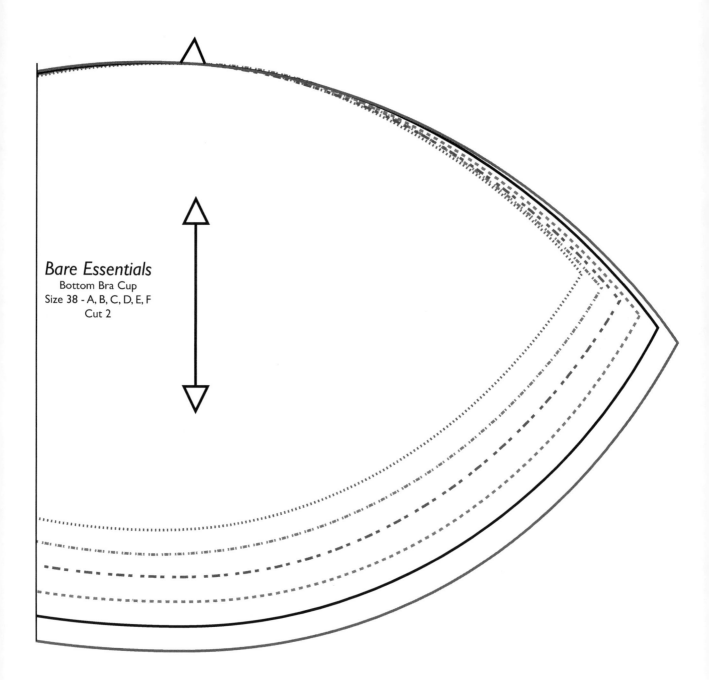

Bare Essentials
Bottom Bra Cup
Size 38 - A, B, C, D, E, F
Cut 2

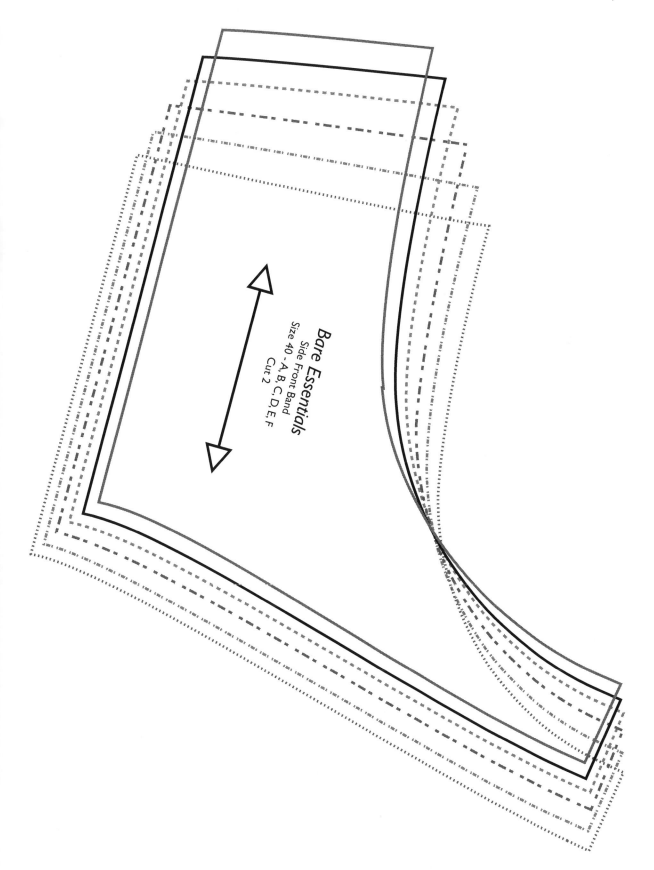

Bare Essentials
Side Front Band
Size 40 - A, B, C, D, E, F
Cut 2

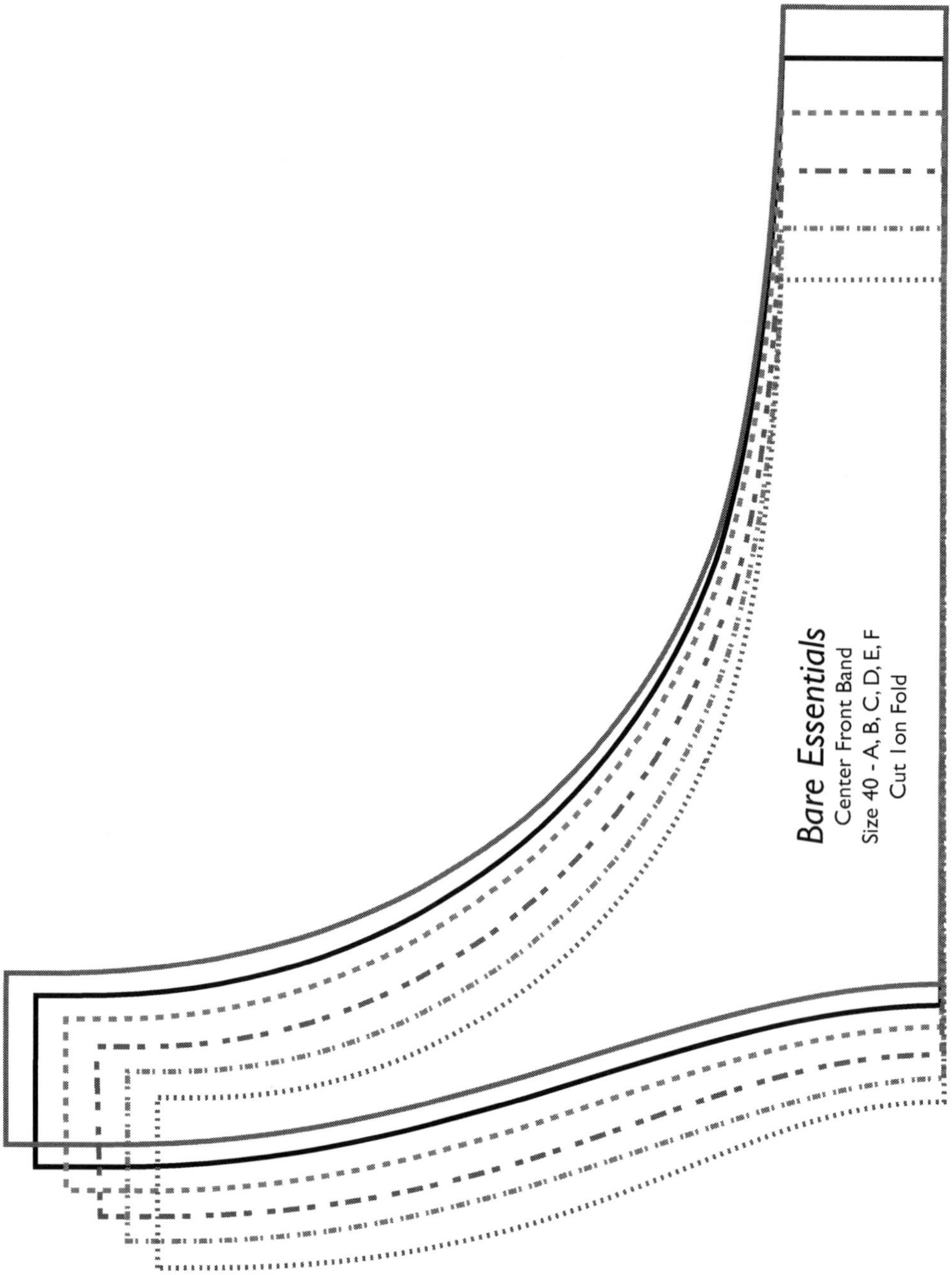

Bare Essentials
Center Front Band
Size 40 - A, B, C, D, E, F
Cut Ion Fold

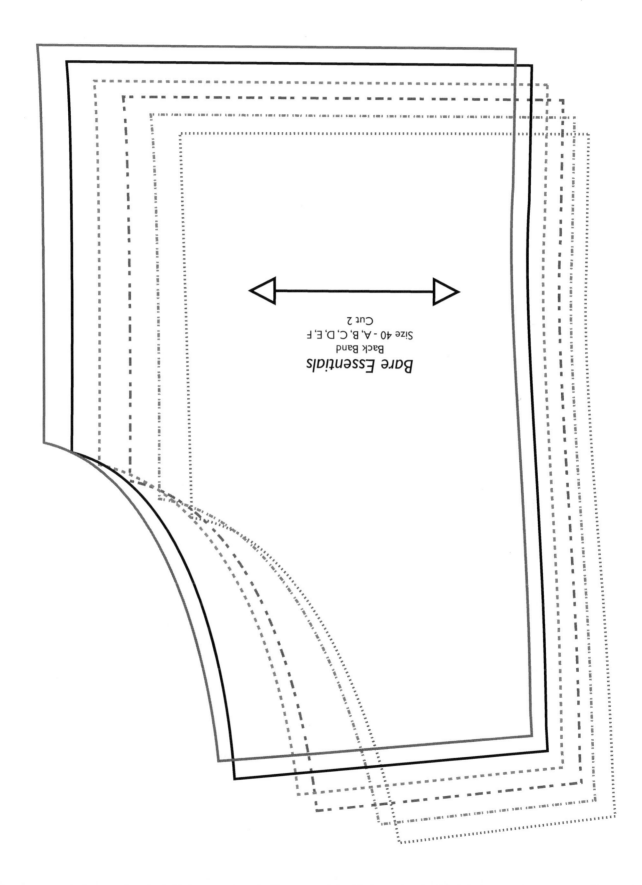

Bare Essentials
Back Band
Size 40 - A, B, C, D, E, F
Cut 2

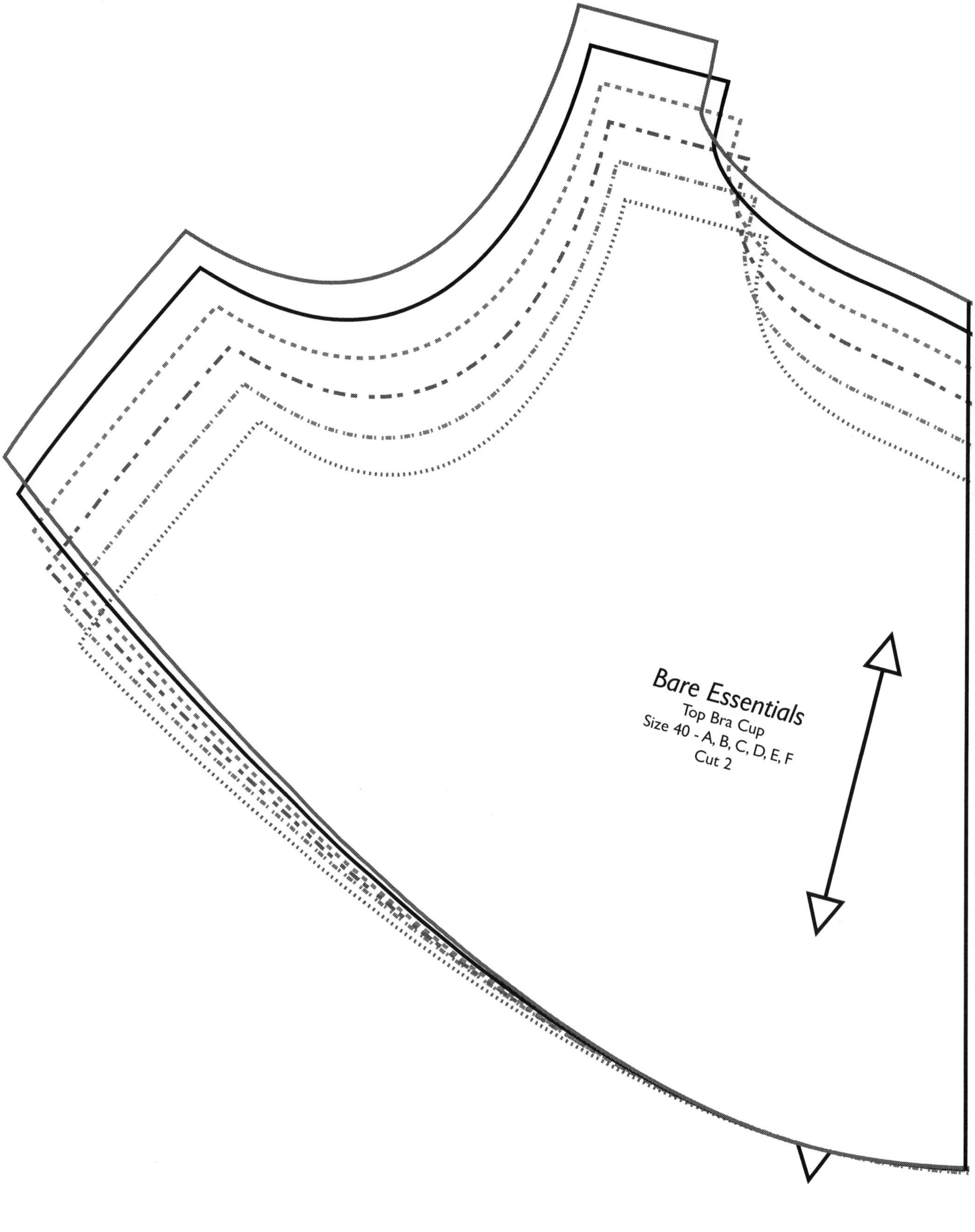

Bare Essentials
Top Bra Cup
Size 40 - A, B, C, D, E, F
Cut 2

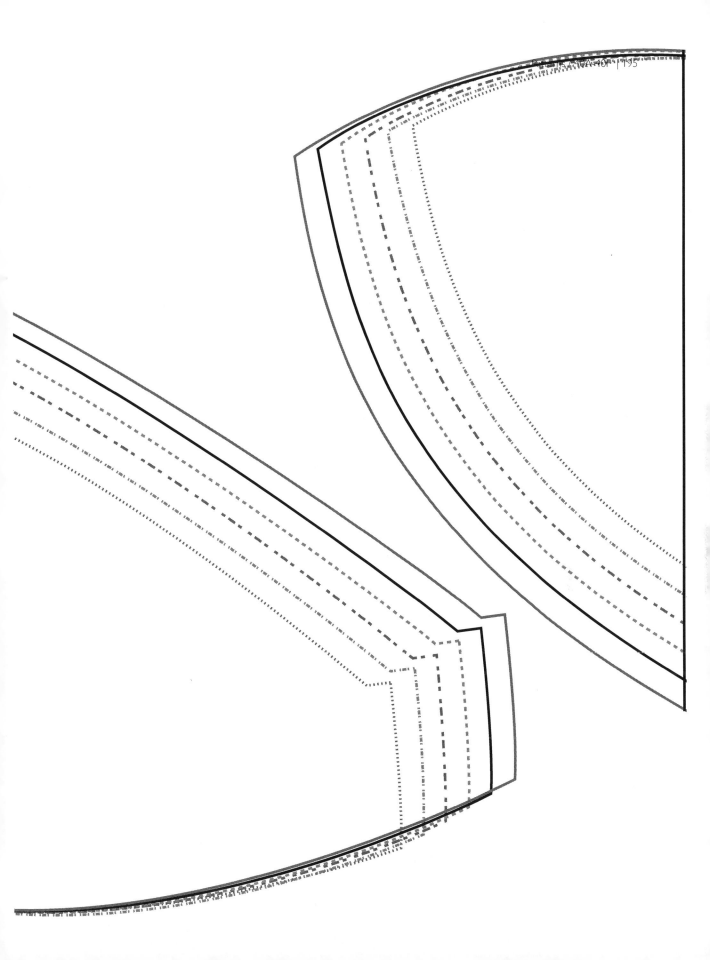

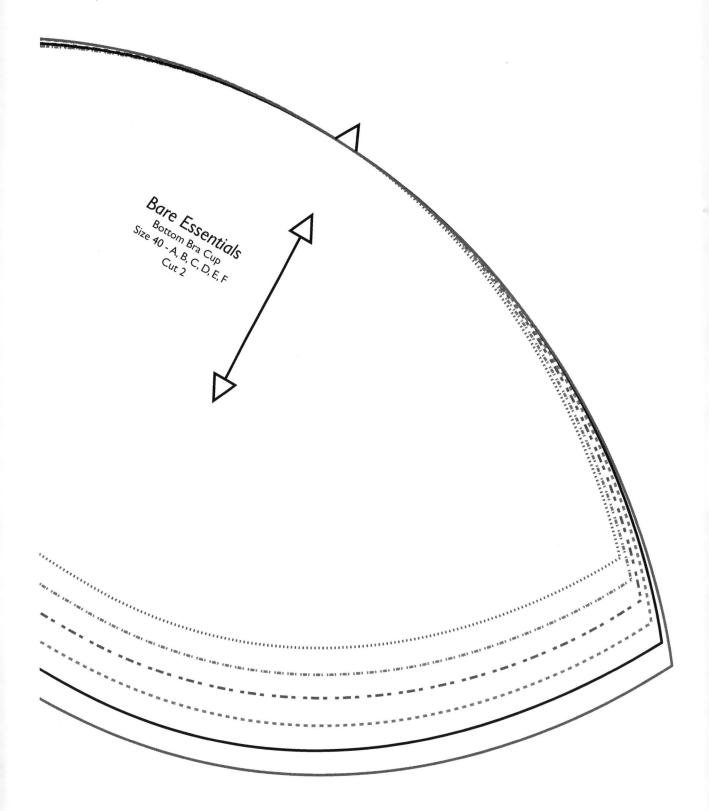

Bare Essentials
Bottom Bra Cup
Size 40 - A, B, C, D, E, F
Cut 2

4100237R00115

Printed in Germany
by Amazon Distribution
GmbH, Leipzig